PUBLIC OPINION,
POLLS,
AND
DEMOCRACY

About the Book and Author

What do public opinion polls really measure? Can polls objectively capture and report public opinion, or do they merely provide data for others to manipulate? Irving Crespi, former executive vice president of The Gallup Organization, offers a critique of the polling enterprise from an insider's point of view. His suggestions for enhancing the democratic function of public opinion polls range from informing the public's understanding of polling methods to reforming the ways in which poll results are reported by the media.

This is one of the first books to examine the 1988 election in light of the media's particular focus on polls. It is also one of the only attempts to link technical and philosophical concerns about the ways, means, and ends of polling. Crespi traces the evolution of polls over the last half century and compares their original conception with their function today. Proceeding on the premise that "polls are here to stay," Crespi devotes a chapter to showing who uses polls and why, with examples drawn from business and interest groups as well as from government and political campaigns. A special chapter treats the nonspecialist to a jargon-free discussion of sampling error, bias, and validity as well as question wording and sequence.

Ideal as a brief and accessible introduction to courses on elections, public opinion, polling, mass media, and political communication, *Public Opinion, Polls, and Democracy* will appeal to those in a variety of disciplines concerned with using polls to promote dialogue among voters, candidates, and public officials.

Irving Crespi is director of media and public affairs research for Total Research Corporation in Princeton, New Jersey. He was affiliated with The Gallup Organization for twenty years, most recently holding the position of executive vice president. He has also served as a polling consultant to the *New York Times,* special adviser to NBC News, and vice president of The Roper Organization. He is coauthor of *Polls, Television, and the New Politics* and is a member of the editorial board of *Public Opinion Quarterly.*

PUBLIC OPINION,
POLLS,
AND
DEMOCRACY

IRVING CRESPI

Foreword by Albert H. Cantril

WESTVIEW PRESS
Boulder • San Francisco • London

Copyright © 1989 by Westview Press, Inc.

Published in 1989 in the United States of America by Westview Press, Inc., 5500 Central Avenue, Boulder, Colorado 80301, and in the United Kingdom by Westview Press, Inc., 13 Brunswick Centre, London WC1N 1AF, England

Library of Congress Cataloging-in-Publication Data
Crespi, Irving.
  Public opinion, polls, and democracy / Irving Crespi.
    p. cm.
  Includes index.
  ISBN 0-8133-0898-4   ISBN 0-8133-0899-2 (pbk.)
  1. Public opinion polls. 2. Democracy. 3. Public opinion—United
States. 4. United States—Politics and government—20th century.
I. Title.
HM261.C69 1989
303.3'8—dc20   89-35021
                                                                       CIP

Printed and bound in the United States of America

⊗   The paper used in this publication meets the requirements of the American National
    Standard for Permanence of Paper for Printed Library Materials Z39.48-1984.

10   9   8   7   6   5   4   3   2

CONTENTS

Tables and Figures

Tables

Figures

FOREWORD

"The obvious weakness of government by opinion is the difficulty of ascertaining it. The more completely popular sovereignty prevails in a country, so much the more important is it that the organs of opinion should be adequate to its expression." Thus it was in the *American Commonwealth* that James Bryce framed the challenge of establishing and nurturing a democratic form of government.

Although Bryce never lived to see the advent of modern public opinion research, his influence on one pioneer of polling, George Gallup, was immense. In Gallup's view, the public opinion poll was to be a foil to entrenched private interests—a way to leaven discourse in the corridors of power with an appropriate respect for the majority view. This orientation has prevailed for half a century as the philosophical bedrock justifying the dogged efforts of pollsters to measure public sentiment.

Yet, some pollsters and many observers of the political scene are nervous that this formulation may be inadequate to the environment of contemporary politics and public affairs. The ubiquity of "the polls" in the 1988 election led thoughtful commentators to wonder whether the nature of public opinion itself was being changed by the incessant drumbeat of poll results. It is a safe guess that more than five hundred "horse race" poll reports appeared in the course of the 1988 presidential campaign, with countless additional polls about state and local races. So many polls, the argument goes, must necessarily affect the way the electorate followed the campaign. And, although less conspicuous between elections, it is feared that the polls facilitate the manipulation of public opinion by interests competing to set the political agenda rather than remind politicians of the underlying reality of public sensibilities.

Thus, it is especially timely to have this inquiry by Irving Crespi. He brings to the task a unique mix of academic grounding and practical experience. His analysis, replete with anecdotes and pertinent illustrations, is inviting to the interested lay reader. Yet polling practitioners can also benefit from Crespi's thoughtful consideration of the many ways a poll can misrepresent public opinion.

Crespi's approach to the polls is holistic as it explores the reciprocal influences of polling, politics, and the media. Crespi pinpoints the consequences, both good and ill, of the pervasiveness of media sponsorship of polls. He reminds us of the complexity and dynamic nature of public opinion that are so often slighted in these polls. He is articulate on the inappropriateness of a "pseudoelection context" for the measurement of opinion on substantive matter and public concerns as, for example, in pressing for an up-down opinion on some complexity in East-West relations as though a vote on the issue were at hand.

Crespi offers sensible recommendations as to how the polls can do a better job capturing the many and changing dimensions of public opinion. Yet, in the end, he is not sanguine that incentives exist for media-sponsored polls—the most visible forms of opinion measurement—to improve much in the years ahead.

So, Lord Bryce's quandary remains with us. But the reader of these pages will come away with a deeper and more subtle understanding of what it will take for the polls truly to serve the democratic process.

Albert H. Cantril
Cambridge, Massachusetts

1
POLLS AND PUBLIC OPINION

What I want is to get done what the people desire to have done, and the question for me is how to find that out exactly.
>—Abraham Lincoln

The study of public opinion has developed from a glorified kind of fortunetelling into a practical way of learning what the nation thinks.
>—George Gallup and Saul Rae

Public opinion polling as we know it today came into being in the middle of the 1930s. In 1935, George Gallup, a former Iowa journalism professor who had come to New York to head the research department of the advertising agency Young and Rubicam, founded the American Institute of Public Opinion (Gallup Poll), a syndicated newspaper feature based on periodic national samplings of public opinion. Almost simultaneously, Elmo Roper, a former jewelry salesman turned marketing researcher, was commissioned by *Fortune* magazine to conduct national polls of public opinion that came to be known as the Fortune Poll. The next year, as interest in the 1936 presidential election mounted, the newspaper syndicate King Features asked Archibald Crossley, who as a Princeton undergraduate had volunteered for military service in World War I before graduation and had then become a marketing researcher, to conduct a series of polls on the election.

Previously, newspapers and magazines had used *straw polls*—sidewalk interviews with haphazardly selected respondents or mail surveys of

1

available lists such as magazine subscribers—to supplement conventional news coverage of elections.[1] The polls conducted by Gallup, Roper, and Crossley differed from those straw polls in that they were based on relatively small but, it was claimed, scientifically selected representative samples of the public. These first modern pollsters further maintained that their poll results—in sharp contrast with the highly personal, impressionistic assessments that politicians, journalists, and political analysts had always relied on—could be treated as scientifically reliable measurements of public opinion.

Since the 1930s, polls have replaced hit-or-miss soundings of opinion made by political reporters and have become a staple feature of political journalism, especially during election years. Polls have also become an essential tool of political consultants in running election campaigns and, to a lesser degree, of lobbyists in seeking to influence policy decisionmakers. Nonetheless, from their beginnings polls have been the target of intense criticism that continues unabated to the present.

THREE TYPES OF CRITICISMS OF POLLS

Much of the criticism directed at polls comes from social scientists, who fault them for two distinct reasons. First, many social scientists contend that the pollsters' underlying assumptions about the nature of public opinion are wrong. These critics assert that a completely different approach to studying public opinion is needed. Second, social scientists charge that the methods used by pollsters—their sampling techniques, question wordings, and analytical procedures—are defective and/or superficial. Those who make this criticism ask for the overhaul of poll methodology and the adoption of state-of-the-art methods that have been developed by social scientists.

A third concern, voiced by many politicians, political analysts, and policymakers and by some members of the general public, has to do with how political life is affected by polls. The issue for these critics is the *ways polls are used* and how these uses have reshaped politics. Their criticisms go beyond issues of theory and methodology to the substantive question of whether polls strengthen or weaken democracy.

We will deal with all three types of criticisms—the nature of public opinion, methods, and uses—with the end purpose of exploring ways in which public opinion polls can add to the vitality of democratic life. For this purpose, we will seek to evaluate the role polls actually play in contemporary politics (Chapter 2), the methodological underpinnings of that role (Chapter 3), and the challenge of how to disseminate poll results in a responsible and constructive manner (Chapter 4). To provide a necessary perspective, we start with a brief review of the controversy that surrounded public opinion polls in their early years and how that controversy continues.

THE ROLE OF PUBLIC OPINION
IN REPRESENTATIVE DEMOCRACIES

George Gallup and political scientist Lindsay Rogers were two of the most outspoken adversaries in the early years of polling. Gallup argued his position in *The Pulse of Democracy*[2] whereas Rogers's criticisms were presented in *The Pollsters.*[3] Underlying their conflict was a fundamental difference in political values that define what should be the role of public opinion in a democracy ruled by elected representatives. Gallup believed in the collective wisdom of ordinary people and distrusted political intellectuals and experts. Rogers felt the need for an enlightened leadership that would rise above the narrow interests, passions, and ignorance of the public at large.

Gallup looked back nostalgically to a time when, presumably, direct democracy prevailed, that is, a time when people ruled themselves by voting directly on all matters—for example, the New England town meeting in colonial times. As he saw it, the problem that faces democracy in representative democracies is how to make the people's representatives properly responsive to the public's wishes and wants. He felt that without the direct expression of public opinion in government, representative democracies would degenerate into government by elites.

Gallup claimed that poll results can be considered a "mandate from the people" that should be followed by the nation's leaders because those results represent what the people want—what legislation they favor, what they oppose, and what policy directions they want the government to follow. Interpreting the intent of the electorate as expressed in elections would no longer be a matter of debate and controversy but something objectively ascertained through polls. Furthermore, when trying to determine the desires and preferences of their constituencies on new issues that arise between elections, legislators would no longer be dependent upon claims of competing special interest groups, newspaper editorials, the mail they receive, or the imperfect soundings they made themselves during visits home. Now they could turn to the latest poll readings to find out what the public really wants.

Gallup further questioned relying exclusively on elections to ensure democratic government, claiming that "Democracy is a process of constant thought and action on the part of the citizen."[4] He concluded that polls can compensate for the limitations of elections in a society in which direct democracy is not feasible. With polls, "legislators, educators, experts, and editors, as well as ordinary citizens . . . , can have a more reliable measure of the pulse of democracy."[5]

The old argument that government should be responsive to public opinion in a representative democracy was given a new saliency by the contention that poll results are trustworthy measurements of public opinion. The proper role of political leaders in a democracy, according to this view, is to be responsive to the will of the people and that political leaders should in effect serve as proxies for their constituents in Congress and other legislative bodies. The public opinion poll was to be welcomed, therefore, as an objective, reliable tool for determining the will of the people. Samuel Stouffer, a sociologist who was also a pioneer in the use of surveys to study attitudes and opinions, agreed, asserting that polls "represent the most useful instrument of democracy ever devised."[6]

Rogers was in direct conflict with Gallup, holding the belief that the hallmark of political leadership in a representative democracy is responsibility to the needs of the commonwealth and not the self-serving wants and often uninformed opinions of individual voters. He cited, with strong approval, Edmund Burke's letter to the people of Bristol, England, the classic eighteenth century statement that in a representative democracy it is the duty of a representative to vote his conscience and not merely to vote as instructed by his constituents.[7] Agreeing with Burke, Rogers argued that we need political leaders who are capable of rising above the narrow self-interest of their constituents and their current but transient opinions, that we need leaders who are motivated by more than the desire to get elected and reelected. He asserted that what we should demand of our political leaders is responsibility to the "true" public interest, not unthinking responsiveness to the narrow self-interests of the voters who elected them. Setting public policy and enacting legislation, he continued, should and must take place through a deliberative process, not by referral to the snap judgments of an uninformed and uninterested public. Polling the public to ascertain what policies it favors, it follows, is an exercise in misguided futility.

Intrinsic to Rogers's understanding of responsible political leadership is the contention that the commonwealth is an organic community and not merely the sum of the individuals who constitute its electorate. Illustrative of this view is the distinction made by the political journalist and philosopher Walter Lippmann between "The People, as voters, [and] *The People*, as a community of the entire living population, with their predecessors and successors." Lippmann maintained that it is often assumed, but without warrant, that the opinions of The People as voters can be treated as the expression of the interests of *The People* as an historic community. The crucial problem of modern democracy arises from the fact that this assumption is false. The voters cannot be relied on to represent *The People*. The opinions of voters in elections are not to be accepted unquestioningly as true judgments of the vital interests of the community. . . . Because of the discrepancy of The People as voters and *The People* as the corporate nation, the voters have no title to consider themselves the proprietors of the commonwealth and to claim that their interests are identical with the public interest.[8]

From this perspective, the governing process in a democracy involves a complex interaction among the executive—"the active power in the state, the asking and the proposing power"; the representative assembly—"the consenting power"; and the voters—who elect the representative assembly.[9]

Lippmann further asserted that effective government is based on negotiations between the executive leadership and the representative assembly, with the voters relegated to a background role: "The government will be refused the means of governing if it does not listen to the petitions, if it does not inform, if it does not consult, if it cannot win the consent of, those who have been elected as the representatives of the governed."[10] In contrast with Gallup's conceptualization of what public opinion is like, Lippmann argued that the public is not a thinking organism and therefore in itself cannot develop programs and policies. What is necessary, according to Lippmann, is that "the program shall be verbally and emotionally connected at the start with what has become vocal in the multitude."[11] Although leaders must pay attention to popular feelings, their responsibility in setting and implementing policy is to act on the basis of their own deliberations.

THE DEBATE ABOUT POLLS
AS VALID MEASURES OF PUBLIC OPINION

Gallup's perspective on public opinion reflected both his early background in journalism and his interest in public opinion as a democratizing force in political life. He described the purpose of the Gallup Poll as performing "the function of fact finding in the realm of opinion in the same general way as the Associated Press, the United Press and the International News Service in the realm of events." He added that polls "improve and objectify the reporting of what people think."[12] He also felt that while in totalitarian countries public opinion may be intangible, "the kind of public opinion implied in the democratic ideal is tangible and dynamic."[13] To him, public opinion is something real that exists ready to be measured objectively. Therefore, if you ask your questions of a valid cross-section of the general public, you have a valid measure of the public's thinking on that topic at that time.

Even when, for the sake of argument, early critics of polls granted that the demands and preferences of the public constitute one set of factors that political leaders should consider, they still questioned the ability of polls to provide valid information about public opinion. To them, public opinion is a quality of the political environment as intangible as the air we breathe and not susceptible to what they claimed were crude "measurements" of a pseudoscience. They considered nonsensical the claim that tallying the number of people who in a poll say they favor or oppose some proposed legislation tells us anything meaningful about public opinion. Rogers was typical in his assertion that not only were significant qualities of public opinion— such as its informational base, intensity, and relationship to group memberships and interests—ignored by pollsters, but that those qualities are not measurable in any meaningful sense. In support of his view that polls do not deal meaningfully with public opinion, he maintained that although pollsters claim they measure it, they cannot define it.[14]

Herbert Blumer, a sociological pioneer in the study of collective behavior, was more willing than Rogers to grant the ability of polls to measure individual opinion but was equally harsh in his assessment of the meaningfulness of such measurements: "Current public opinion polling necessarily operates with a conception of public opinion that is a gross distortion. By virtue of its sampling procedure, current public opinion polling is forced to regard public opinion as an aggregate of equally weighted opinions of disparate individuals. . . . Public opinion is organic and not an aggregate of equally weighted opinions."[15] Blumer argued that public opinion must be studied in the "social framework in which it moves," with a focus on the activities of organized groups that operate within that framework. In his view, measuring and adding up individual opinions, as is done in polling, tells us nothing about how public opinion actually functions in real life.[16]

Other social scientists, while acknowledging that polling as conducted in its formative years had serious limitations, defended the intrinsic value of the method for determining public opinion. Julian Woodward, who served as a consultant to Roper, pointed out that the meaningfulness of counting individual opinions is based on the model of the voting booth.[17] Theodore Newcombe, a social psychologist, concurring in this view, went on to observe that there is no methodological reason polls could not analyze the social context of individual opinions, the intensity with which they are held, or the processes through which they come into existence and express themselves.[18]

As experience with polling accumulated, some social scientists concluded that rather than lacking validity, polls have enriched our understanding of how public opinion functions in the political life of the United States. Robert Erickson and Norman Luttbeg asserted that the inexact, qualitative, intuitive methods used prior to the development of scientific polling to find out what the public was thinking—consulting friends, tabulating mail to political officeholders and to newspapers, gauging reactions of crowds to political oratory, and even analyzing election outcomes—had substantial biases built into them. Erickson and Luttbeg also observed that polls have "focused our attention to the fact that the various devices of public expression available in a democracy were not channeling an accurate reflection of public opinion to public decision makers."[19] Citing poll results that documented the inattentiveness, ignorance, and lack of awareness of large segments of the public, they concluded that assumptions about the active role public opinion is expected to play in a democracy must be reexamined.

POPULISM, MASS SOCIETY, AND POLLS

The contrast between a belief in the concrete reality of public opinion and the view that public opinion is an intangible quality of an organic community has been bridged by Leo Bogart, an analyst of mass communications. He pointed out that accepting polls as a valid method for investigating public opinion entails a redefinition of what we mean by the term *public opinion* and what role it can and should play in politics. He noted that although public opinion had historically been discussed as "one force among many in the complex flux of politics . . . capricious and unpredictable like an air or ocean current," poll methodology "requires that these elusive currents be treated as though they were static, that we define and measure what was previously undefinable and unmeasurable."[20] That is to say, reliance on public opinion polls is associated with a transition in the character and quality of public opinion that is in turn associated with larger societal changes in education and communications systems. Gallup also stressed the way in which the nature of public opinion has changed along with other changes in social structure: "Public opinion is not today, as it was then [at the founding of the Republic], the opinion of a small and exclusive minority of educated persons enjoying a monopoly of economic and political power."[21] We can add to the insight that public opinion is a historical phenomenon, changing in nature as the sociopolitical context changes, by analyzing the rise of polling as part of a twofold process of political change—one related to populism and the other to mass politics.

A long-term trend in U.S. politics is the increased access of the general public to all aspects of political activity. This trend includes, most importantly, the gradual elimination of limitations on the right to vote. Thus, restrictions based on property ownership, religion, residence requirements, literacy tests, sex, poll taxes, race, and age have either been eliminated or weakened. Additionally, referenda on public issues, such as the California proposition on automobile insurance and the Maryland proposition on gun control in 1988, have on occasion become as important a part of state and local elections as is voting for candidates for public office. Another major development is that primaries have increasingly replaced party conventions and caucuses as the mechanism through which candidates for office are selected.

There is a strong *populist* strain—a faith in the wisdom of the ordinary citizen to make sound decisions—in all these developments. This populism is also intrinsic to public opinion polling as conceived by such pioneers as Gallup. In developing his justification for public opinion polls, Gallup observed that "it [public opinion] believes in the value of every individual's contribution to political life, and in the right of ordinary human beings to have a voice in deciding their fate. Public opinion, in this sense, is the pulse of democracy."[22]

A frequent populist argument in support of polling is that elections are an incomplete basis for assessing public opinion. Jerome S. Bruner, one of the early academic users of polls, observed that whereas elections are the payoff in a democracy, letters to members of Congress and newspapers and participation in mass meetings and rallies have been traditional channels for expressing public opinion.[23] In common with other proponents of polling, Bruner also pointed out that these channels favor organized groups representing vested interests. Polls, he maintained, act to redress the balance by giving ordinary citizens a means for making their voices heard: "In the past, . . . it has been the custom to discuss public opinion *only* in terms of organized groups. . . . And so if polls are on the side of taking people in their abstract mass, the error has the virtue of egalitarian intent, of balancing one-sided impressions cultivated by the 'pressure boys.'"[24]

Gallup conceded that the first and most important index of public opinion is elections, but he also felt strongly that we cannot rely solely upon elections to discover what the public wants. He maintained that voting decisions are as much a reflection of attitudes regarding the personal qualities of candidates as opinions on issues and that successful candidates unwarrantedly assumed that their election was a blanket endorsement of their stand on all issues.[25]

According to the most committed adherents of polls, they are a tool for democracy specifically because they do *not* investigate those aspects of organized public opinion that critics such as Rogers and Blumer felt should be of primary interest. Gallup added to this argument the question, "shall the common people be free to express their basic needs and purposes, or shall they be dominated by a small ruling clique?"[26]

Gallup was also concerned that the rise of new forms of communication gives entrenched elites the power to control both the formation and expression of public opinion, so that "the voice of the common man grew faint in the din and clatter of other voices speaking in his name. . . . Public opinion can be a satisfactory guide only if we can hear it and, what is equally important, if it can hear itself."[27] He concluded that "public opinion can only be of service to democracy if it can be heard."[28] This same point has been made more recently by Elisabeth Noelle-Neumann: "Those whose point of view is not represented by the media are effectively mute."[29] M. Margolis has labeled this process whereby public opinion is ignored or made mute one in which public opinion becomes the dependent rather than the independent variable.[30]

Gallup posed two questions that epitomize his justification of polling: "Can democracy develop new techniques to meet the impact of this strange new decade?" "Shall the common people be free to express their basic needs and purposes, or shall they be dominated by a small ruling clique?"[31] He saw public opinion polls as the answer to both these questions: Polls provide both a means through which the public can speak for itself and a bridge between the people and their political leaders that circumvents the pretensions of self-designated spokespersons.[32]

The opposition between the populist view that representatives should be responsive to the opinions of their constituencies and the contention that representatives should exercise their own judgments in as responsible a manner as they can persists in continuing controversy about the value of polls. This opposition was evident in the controversy that followed George Bush's victory in the 1988 presidential election as to what kind of a mandate, if any, he had received. In the days immediately following the election, the major national news media reported the results of polls they had conducted, especially "exit polls" with voters as they left their voting places, in their analyses of what voters had in mind when they cast their ballots and therefore what was their mandate. This reporting was in keeping with the role that polling pioneers such as Gallup wanted polls to have.

As might be expected, the validity of seeking to define a mandate on the basis of polls was challenged. John O'Sullivan, editor of the *National Review,* criticized this use of polls in words reminiscent of Burke, Rogers, and Lippmann:

> The very latest theory of the mandate asserts that what really counts is an opinion given by 1,000 people to a man asking them questions. And since such opinions are changeable, contradictory and of varying significance, someone must select which are political facts. That someone turns out to be the Fourth Estate.
>
> But the mandate, whether it is based on polls or pledges, is alien to a representative government in which a candidate is selected by voters to use his judgment on their behalf. He is not, of course, a completely free agent but acts under two constraints. First, if he has given firm pledges on matters of topical controversy, he cannot honorably abandon them unless a major change of circumstance occurs. Second, he must present his philosophy so that voters may determine how he is likely to use his judgment in situations they cannot forsee.[33]

Those who believe that the duty of elected representatives is to exercise their personal judgments, and not to serve as little more than conduits for the wishes of their constituencies, inevitably reject the notion that polls can be used to identify a public mandate.

In summary, the populist argument for polling, explicitly developed by Gallup but inherent in the underlying assumptions of public opinion polling, is that elections in themselves are an imperfect medium for the expression of public opinion, that without some channel specifically designed for that purpose public opinion will not be an effective force for democracy, and that polls can be used to fulfill that function. Through its claim that polling protects and extends the ability of ordinary citizens to participate meaningfully in the political life of contemporary society, this populist argument provides an ideology to justify polling.

POLITICAL LINKAGE IN MASS SOCIETY

Polling is also a manifestation of increased mass participation in national politics, as distinct from participation through membership in face-to-face community organizations and local political groups.[34] As such, polling is symptomatic of the effects that population growth, urbanization, and the emergence of mass media of communication have had on politics. At one time, party organizations consisted of a network of personal relationships between local precinct leaders and their neighbors out of which emerged county organizations that in turn formed the building blocks of the state parties. The national parties were little more than alliances of state parties that were activated every four years to elect a president. The interests, desires, and preferences of the public were communicated to political leaders largely through personal access to this network.

Today, other than voting, ordinary citizens participate in politics primarily in two ways: as part of mass audiences that passively follow the news as reported on television and in mass circulation newspapers and magazines and, more actively, as members of and/or contributors to mass organizations and movements. Contributing to a political action committee, or responding to the mail appeals of special interest lobbies headquartered in Washington, is very different from contacting one's precinct captain or attending local political meetings and rallies. The former are individual acts, socially isolated in that they do not involve face-to-face relationships; they epitomize life in mass society. The latter enmesh the individual in a network of interpersonal relationships. By treating public opinion as the sum of the opinions of the *individuals* who make up the electorate, rather than as a force that emerges from organized society, pollsters implicitly, if not explicitly, define their task as the measurement of public opinion in mass society.

Populist proponents of polling have assumed that polls strengthen the voices of common citizens in mass society when political leaders decide what public policy should be and how that policy should be implemented. Skepticism about this assumption has long been voiced even by those who accept the validity of polls. An early skeptic was Leonard Doob, a social psychologist who during World War II served in a number of government agencies in which he was able to observe the use of poll results by decisionmakers. On the basis of his experience in government, Doob described polls as "a measuring instrument dedicated to very practical and useful objectives . . . [for] determining short-range facts about people and in measuring their attitudes after an issue has produced actual public opinion."[35] He found that those government officials who relied on poll results to evaluate public reactions to government programs did so only to help them implement policies that had already been decided: "Polls serve not to formulate overall policy but merely to help determine specific sub-policies which are really only means to predetermined ends."[36]

Doob also called attention to the use of poll results by lobbyists seeking to propagate public support for their positions.[37] Agreeing that polls can tell us what the public is thinking, Doob still cautioned that they do not automatically further democractic political processes. His early, perspicacious assessment of the potentially dark side of polling calls our attention to the critical questions of how polls are actually utilized by contemporary political leaders and whether that utilization has strengthened or weakened democracy.

The issue thus becomes one of *political linkage*—that is, the "means by which political leaders act in accordance with the wants, needs and demands of the public in making government policy."[38] This raises the question as to what kind of linkage is assumed by polling. To deal with this question, let us consider three models of linkage: (1) *the rationalist-activist model* in which average citizens—politically informed, involved, and rational—form personal opinions that they express through voting and communications to their representatives in government, (2) *the political parties model* in which the ties between the public and political leaders are institutionalized and are therefore subject to processes that can distort or muffle public opinion, and (3) *the pressure groups model* according to which the public develops, expresses, and acts upon its opinions through organized groups.[39]

Conducting polls to implement a populist ideology conforms to the rationalist-activist model. Distrustful of parties and pressure groups, pollsters such as Gallup argued that true democracy is enhanced when polls give voice to ordinary citizens whose judgment on public issues can be relied on as informed and reasoned. The possibility that polls might strengthen linkages between the public and political leaders through parties or through pressure groups was not considered by those early pollsters. They assumed, uncritically, that polls would inevitably strengthen rationalist-activist linkages. This is an assumption that we shall question—and reject.

THE PLAN OF THIS BOOK

Identifying the populist roots of polling and polling's relevance to the emergence of mass politics does not answer the arguments of critics who maintain that (1) polling is based on a misconception of the true nature of public opinion, (2) effective representative democracy requires a responsible leadership that does not blindly follow the twists and reversals of a fickle public opinion, and (3) trying to capture the ineffable essence of public opinion through sample surveys is an exercise in futility. Moreover, whether polling has, in fact, strengthened democracy in our mass society or whether its critics are correct in saying that it has perverted traditional concepts of representative democracy is a serious question to consider. Although these issues must be central to any examination of the role that polls play in contemporary politics, I shall not deal with them directly. Instead, I will adopt a more descriptive strategy that will, ultimately, enable us to resolve these issues.

My starting point is the fact that for better or for worse, polls have become an integral part of contemporary politics and that it is highly unlikely that the prominence of polls in politics will decline in the foreseeable future. To the contrary, polls are playing an expanding (some would say dominating) rather than a contracting role in political life. Given this reality, debating whether polls measure "real" public opinion and whether we should pay any attention to polls seems a rather sterile exercise. Instead, I propose to do three things:

1. Examine (in Chapter 2) as carefully as possible how polls are and are not actually being used—as distinct from what pollsters have said about how they are intended to be used. Doing this will enable us to determine the actual political significance of polls regardless of their ideological acceptability. Instead of asking, "What do we say we want polls to do?" we shall ask, "What are we actually using polls for?"

2. Evaluate (in Chapter 3) the validity of the methods currently employed by pollsters in relation to the uses to which polls *are* being put. Instead of asking whether polls really measure some preconceived notion of public opinion, we can better ask, "Are polls being conducted in ways that provide relevant information that can be used with confidence by those who actually use them?" Answering this question will require a review of the methodological principles that underly polling, although a detailed technical exposition will not be attempted. (There is a voluminous literature on survey methodology that should be consulted by those seeking to learn how to conduct polls.) We will then be able to evaluate how survey methodology must be employed if polls are to produce meaningful and valid information about public opinion.

3. Seek (in Chapter 4) an answer to the question, "Given the likelihood that public opinion polls will continue to play a prominent role in politics, what can be done to maximize their positive contributions to the political process?" It is very easy to document instances in which polls have been misused and abused. Learning to use polls in a socially useful manner is far more difficult. If we have to live with polls, and that seems to be the reality, rather than only criticize their faults we should devote our efforts to finding out how they can be used to further representative democracy.

2
HOW POLLS ARE USED

In a representative democracy, public opinion's most direct effect is on elections. Thus, it is not surprising that public opinion polls have, from their beginning, been most closely associated with elections. Whatever purposes pollsters have ascribed to their activities, public interest in polls has always centered on whether they can accurately predict who will win an election.

The early acceptance of polls conducted by Gallup, Roper, and Crossley was based primarily, if not completely, on their correct forecasts in 1936 of a comfortable Roosevelt victory, which contradicted the prediction of the then-prestigious *Literary Digest* Poll that Alfred Landon would win. Public acceptance of polls as a journalistic feature during the next decade was the result of the record compiled by some preelection polls in correctly indicating the winners in presidential and other elections. However, the polls' failure to anticipate Harry Truman's upset victory over Thomas Dewey in 1948 created a crisis that some feared would threaten the existence not only of public opinion polls but of all applications of the survey method.

In the wake of the 1948 polling fiasco, many newspapers canceled their subscriptions to the Gallup Poll, and a number of clients of Gallup's then-thriving movie research business canceled or refused to renew contracts.[1] Roper was in a more favorable position because his polling was conducted for only one client, *Fortune*, which continued its sponsorship for a while longer. Nevertheless, Roper's commercial marketing research business suffered a contraction, temporary but sharp, in the immediate aftermath of his 1948 miscall.[2] Concern about the loss of credibility of all surveys spread into the academic community and led the Social Science Research Council (a nonprofit organization that funds social science research) to investigate the factors that accounted for the failure of the 1948 polls.[3]

The road back to public acceptance was long and difficult. Not until after the 1960 election—in which every poll indicated either that John Kennedy would win in a close election or that if Richard Nixon did win, the margin would be quite small—did polling regain widespread public confidence. That is, the restoration of public confidence in polls was dependent upon the perceived accuracy of preelection polls. Today, preelection polling remains a significant focus of media-sponsored polls, including the major national polls (Gallup, Harris, CBS/*New York Times,* ABC/*Washington Post,* NBC/*Wall Street Journal, Los Angeles Times,* Roper/*U.S. News,* and *USA Today*/Gordon Black) as well as myriad state and local polls. Any examination of the way public opinion polls are used must start with the role of preelection polls.

PREELECTION POLLS

Since 1948, pollsters have repeatedly emphasized that preelection polls are not predictions but are snapshots of the sum of voting intentions at specified points in time (an assertion whose validity, as we shall see later, has been verified). Nonetheless, interest in preelection polls is based on the belief that they provide accurate measures of how the electorate is tending in its voting intentions. Even polls conducted a year or more in advance of an election are typically treated as predictions. For example, "In 1985, he [Mayor Edward Koch of New York] won seventy-eight percent of the vote in the general election. According to a *Times*/WCBS-TV poll, taken in late June [1988], only twenty-seven percent of New Yorkers would vote for him again [in 1989]."[4] Politicians, journalists, and the general public alike have come to rely on preelection polls as indicators of what is likely to happen on Election Day, that is, as indicators of what a future event will be. Other topics covered by opinion polls—issues of the day, human interest stories, or the public's concerns and aspirations—have not been able to generate as much general interest as does finding out what will be the nation's political future.

Poll Topics in Nonelection Years

Given that elections are not held every day, pollsters are under considerable business pressure to develop other poll topics that will

TABLE 2.1
Early Gallup Questions Designed to Measure Political Strength in Nonelection Years

Trial Heat

"What candidate for Congress from your district do you think you will vote for in the next congressional election—the Democratic candidate, the Republican candidate, or another party's candidate?" (10/30–11/4/1937)

"If Harry Hopkins runs for President in 1940 on the Democratic ticket against Thomas Dewey on the Republican ticket, which candidate would you prefer?" (1/22–27/1939)

Mock Primaries

(Asked of Democrats) "If President Roosevelt is not a candidate in 1940, who do you think will make the best Democratic candidate?" (3/12–17/1937)

(Asked of Republicans) "Who do you think will make the best Republican candidate in 1940?" (4/21–26/1937)

Party Identification

Do you regard yourself as a Republican, a Democrat, a Socialist, or an Independent in politics?" (3/3–8/1937)

Presidential Popularity

"In general, do you approve or disapprove of Franklin Roosevelt as President?" (5/20–25/1939)

Most Capable Party

"Which political party do you think is more likely to keep us out of war—the Republican or the Democratic?" (12/2–7/1939)

Source: George Gallup, *The Gallup Poll: Public Opinion, 1935–1971* (New York: Random House, 1972), pp. 54, 59, 60, 77, 141, 157, 194.

generate comparable interest (and therefore comparable income) during nonelection years. In his search for such topics, Gallup invented a number of questions that have become the bread and butter of political polling in the long periods between formal election campaigns. (Table 2.1 lists questions asked by Gallup in the nonelection years 1937 and 1939. Somewhat differently worded questions are now used by the Gallup Poll.) These include *trial heats,* which ask for preference between possible contenders for office in future elections; *mock primaries,* which ask for preference among various possible contenders for nomination to office; and *approval* or popularity questions, which ask how satisfied the electorate is with the performance in office of incumbents.[5]

Although these three types of questions differ in their specifics, they have one characteristic in common—they provide a pseudoelection context for the poll. Even when there is no election in the immediate offing, these questions each purport to measure political strength as if one were to be held. Since eventually there will be an election, the results of such polls are examined by political analysts as if they were a preview of what may eventually happen. Illustrative of this practice is a report on a CBS News/*New York Times* poll conducted in January 1987, a full year before the 1988 presidential primaries were to begin. That poll was reported to have found Gary Hart "the clear early leader" for the Democratic party's nomination, although Mario Cuomo "could pose a serious challenge" if he were to run; "among Republicans, Vice President Bush leads Bob Dole, the Senate minority leader, by a margin of better than 2 to 1."[6]

Closely related to trial heats, mock primaries, and measures of presidential popularity are questions, also first developed by Gallup, that ask about such matters as political party identification and the ability of each party to best handle important problems of the day. Again, answers to these questions are interpreted by political analysts as clues to future voting behavior. Illustrative of this is a news analysis by Adam Clymer, based on a seven-year trend in party identification as measured in CBS News and *New York Times* polls. Clymer concluded from his analysis that the women's vote could prove critical in the congressional elections to be held six months later in November.[7]

The Emergence of Continuing Elections

In the process of asking such questions, albeit without conscious or inadvertent intent, pollsters slowly created what can best be called *continuing elections.* The basic nature of these continuing elections was clear by the end of the 1960s.

> Candidate preferences, the popularity of incumbents, and the relative standing of parties are measurable every month of every year. . . . In the past, political campaigning was a part-time affair, except for periods of intense activity during the formal campaign. . . . [Today] the trend in the public's evaluation of the politically prominent is measured continually by published polls up to nominating time for the next election. Thus, the politically ambitious person must mature and develop under the pitiless glare of unending public assessment. . . . The effect of this constant measurement upon the electoral process is to make it an *endless event,* with elections as periodic climaxes.[8]

During Ronald Reagan's presidency, the evolution of continuing elections came to full flower. Weekly conferences reviewed the results of privately commissioned polls, particularly those conducted by Richard Wirthlin, and of media-sponsored polls. These conferences evaluated Reagan's personal public standing in relation to prospects for public acceptance of his policies and of the Republican party. As Sidney

Blumenthal described it, the United States was witnessing government by "permanent campaign":

> Ronald Reagan is governing America by a new strategic doctrine—the permanent campaign. He is applying in the White House the techniques he employed in getting there. Making more effective use of media and market research than any previous President, he has brought into the White House the most sophisticated team of pollsters, media masters and tacticians ever to work there. They have helped him to transcend entrenched institutions like the Congress and the Washington press corps to appeal directly to the people.[9]

Government by permanent campaign is effective because politicians assume that popularity ratings and trial heats say something valid about such matters as the reelectability of an incumbent president. Poll ratings thereby influence a president's political clout in legislative battles in a manner that, although less tangible than his ability to offer or withhold political favors, is just as real. Members of Congress can find it very difficult to resist the demands of such a president as Reagan, who was able throughout most of his term of office to maintain a strong personal appeal to the electorate. Conversely, the decline in Jimmy Carter's popularity during his final year in office, as measured by polls, weakened the effectiveness of his administration in dealing with Congress. After Reagan's popularity ratings dropped in the wake of the Iran-contra hearings—as measured by the Gallup Poll question "Do you approve or disapprove of the way Ronald Reagan is handling his job as President?" (his rating dropped from 63 percent to 47 percent in the six-week period from October 1986 to December 1986 and then dropped to 40 percent by February 1987)[10]—his influence in Congress reportedly weakened. On the other hand, George Bush's successful bid for the presidency in 1988 was tied to a partial recovery in Reagan's popularity to 51 percent approve in July 1988.

The Effect of Popularity Ratings

High personal standings in polls can be used to vindicate a president's efforts to implement policies that other poll results suggest do not have majority public support. Public opinion polls conducted during Reagan's second term of office consistently revealed widespread reservations about high levels of military spending and involvement in Central America. Nonetheless, public opposition to those policies apparently weighed less in the assessments of politicians than did the high personal standing Reagan continued to achieve in polls from 1985 through most of 1987. This again illustrates the principle that poll results that are believed to provide information about voting strength have greater political significance than do those that presumably inform us about the public's opinions on specific issues.

That is not to say that politicians and policymakers ignore the public's opinions on issues. They do act when it appears that the public's feelings on an issue are strong enough to weaken popularity ratings. Reagan's handling of Social Security is particularly illustrative. Initially, attempts by Democrats to use his previous criticisms of the Social Security system to weaken Reagan politically appeared to resonate with the public's fears that Social Security was in danger of being phased out. Reagan rapidly defused this issue with repeated pledges to preserve Social Security and to protect existing retirement benefits. In this instance, polls served as an early warning system, identifying the need to take corrective action against developments that could undermine the perception that Reagan's appeal to the electorate was unchallengeable.

Confidence in the ability of polls to predict elections has led to the widespread use of polls in ways that go far beyond predicting elections. When considering the political costs of alternative courses of action, politicians now rely on polls as the single most important source of information about trends in the climate of public opinion, especially as they might affect future voting behavior. When used in this way, poll results are more accurately described as *political intelligence* (information used for planning strategy and tactics) than as policy guides or instructions from the public to its political leaders.

POLLS AS POLITICAL INTELLIGENCE

The extent to which politicians have come to rely on polls for political intelligence becomes graphically evident when poll data are not available. Just before the 1988 South Dakota presidential preference primary, Rick Hauffer, the acting director of the South Dakota Democratic party, was asked to evaluate the likely outcome of that primary. He responded that with no independent polls to guide them, "we are all flying by the seat of our pants. . . . The conventional wisdom is that Gephardt and Dukakis are ahead, but no one can really know until Tuesday's votes are counted."[11]

The Use of Privately Commissioned Polls

When using polls for intelligence, politicians do not rely solely on media-sponsored polls. Instead, they increasingly commission private polls whose results, unless leaked to the press for tactical reasons, remain closely guarded secrets. Although the names of some pollsters who specialize in conducting private polls are well known to political sophisticates—Richard Wirthlin, Robert Teeter, and Lance Tarrance for Republicans and Bill Hamilton, Peter Hart, and Harrison Hickman for Democrats—these names are only the tip of the iceberg. Both the Republican and Democratic National Committees distribute to candidates of their respective parties lists of approved political consultants numbering in the hundreds, many of whom include polling among the services they offer. The 1988–1989 edition of *The Political Resources Directory* lists 168 organizations that conduct polls.[12] Not all conduct private polls (some are academically based), but this listing is by no means exhaustive of all the firms that conduct polls for candidates and parties.

Another numerical indicator of how dependent politicians have become on private polls is the amount of money they spend for this purpose. In 1964, politicians paid an estimated $6 million for private polling; for 1984, the figure has been estimated to be more than $40 million for private polls and approximately $20 million for media-sponsored polls.[13] In part, the increased spending in private polling reflects inflation-related rises in cost. Whereas in 1964 an in-depth national poll cost about $15,000–$25,000,[14] in 1988 one poll based on telephone interviews with a sample of 1,000 respondents cost about $38,000.[15] Nevertheless, after allowing for inflation, there has still been an explosive increase in the volume of private polling since the 1960s.

Polls as the Primary Source of Political Intelligence

The past twenty years has also witnessed the continuing replacement by pollsters of local party politicians and organizations as the primary source of political intelligence.[16] This replacement is an integral part of the declining importance of traditional party organizations in elections specifically and in politics generally. Election campaigns are increasingly managed by professional technocrats—paid campaign managers, advertising agencies, and media experts as well as pollsters—rather than by party loyalists who are compensated by jobs, political favors, and elective offices. The expense of polls—$25,000 is probably the minimum for a single, bare-bones professional poll, and costs can and do run much higher—has added to the cost of being a candidate. This cost cannot be discharged by postelection favors but must be taken care of in advance. (Private pollsters have learned to demand advance payment lest they never get paid at all.)

The increased reliance on polls for political intelligence is also symptomatic of the transformation of precinct and clubhouse politics into mass politics. Communication between political leaders and the general public is channelled less through party organizations whose primary function had historically been the cultivation of personal ties between voters and political parties and more through mass communications. Individual politicians use the mass media to communicate directly to unorganized audiences and use polls to learn about the thinking of those audiences. Although the emergence of mass politics is the result of a number of social trends, such as population growth, urbanization, and technological innovation, polls have played an essential role in the process.

The use of polls as political intelligence is a highly developed activity in the conduct of election campaigns. Three applications stand out: (1) measuring the voting strengths and weaknesses of opposing candidates and the progress of their campaigns; (2) selecting and defining issues on which to campaign; and (3) selecting candidates to support. Let us consider each in turn.

Measuring the Voting Strengths and Weaknesses of Opposing Candidates

Perhaps the single most common use of private polls is to measure the voting strengths and weaknesses of competing candidates. This is a natural extension of the use of polls by news media to predict election outcomes. In the context of private polling, however, the purpose is not to predict but to influence elections. Knowing whether a candidate is ahead or behind, by how much, and how standings differ between demographic segments of the electorate contributes to realistic assessments of what has to be achieved if an election is to be won. This knowledge can be of great value to campaign organizers and strategists in determining intensity of campaigning, in allocating campaign resources, and in targeting campaign efforts to specific populations. When a poll shows a candidate in the lead, campaign managers expect that analyzing the pattern of that lead will enable them to develop strategies that will consolidate and perhaps even increase the indicated margin of victory. Conversely, campaign managers analyze polls for trailing candidates to discover how to overcome their initial disadvantage. In either case, campaign managers expect that a campaign strategy based on knowledge of early candidate standings will result in an improvement in the candidate's voting appeal.

The pollster's role in campaign strategy

The pollster's private role is not only to provide reliable information but also, and at least as importantly, to analyze that information in a way that will contribute to the development of a winning campaign strategy. The private pollster is not a disinterested, objective investigator of the political scene but an integral part of the campaign management team. Richard Wirthlin, who polled for Robert Dole during the 1988 Republican presidential primary campaign, is credited with playing a key role in Dole's decision not to mount an aggressive advertising campaign in the final days before the New Hampshire primary.[17] (Wirthlin was also a key person at weekly White House meetings on political strategy during the Reagan administration.) Similarly, Robert Teeter, who directed the polls conducted for George Bush in 1988, played a major role in deciding Bush's campaign strategy, was credited by some as influencing the selection of Dan Quayle to be Bush's running mate (Teeter had conducted polls for Quayle in previous campaigns), served as co-director of Bush's transition team, and for a while was thought to be a candidate to serve as a co-chief of staff in the Bush White House.

The pollster's role in getting a candidate elected

The success of private pollsters is evaluated not so much by the accuracy with which their polls measure candidate standings as by their contributions to getting their candidates elected. Thus, when describing his methods for identifying likely voters in the private polls he conducts, Peter Hart stated that he was more concerned that he might erroneously include nonvoters in his sample than that he might exclude a few likely voters.[18] This is not to imply that private pollsters have no interest in conducting accurate polls. To the contrary, a private pollster who gets a reputation for inaccuracy is not likely to stay in business very long, and the best private pollsters pride themselves on the sophistication of their methods. Nevertheless, private pollsters do not boast as much about their accuracy (as do Gallup and Harris) as about how many candidates they have helped to win.

The stress on guidance in planning and executing campaigns that characterizes private polls stands in contrast to the emphasis on accurate measurement in media-sponsored polls, which cannot avoid public comment on their accuracy. Thus, although the credibility of private polls initially derived from the accuracy records compiled by media-sponsored polls and from the assumption that similar methods were used by both, the accuracy of private polls is seldom a matter of public record, and private pollsters can to a surprising degree avoid the criterion of accuracy when their work is evaluated.

Selecting and Defining Issues

Using polls to select issues on which to campaign has become about as common as using them to assess voting strength. In this application, polls are used to (1) identify the relative importance of different issues to the electorate, (2) uncover matters of concern to the electorate that may not have received much attention but that could be developed into effective issues, (3) differentiate effective and ineffective arguments for a given issue, and (4) position a candidate on these issues.

Identifying the relative importance of issues

Open-ended questions—for example, "What is the most important problem facing the country today?"—that leave it to respondents to name whatever issues they think of are especially useful for selecting and defining issues. In answer to this question, only 2 percent named drugs in 1986, but 16 percent did in 1988, thus making it the most frequently named problem in that election year. Conversely, unemployment and recession ranked first in frequency of mention in 1986, named by 16 percent, compared with 8 percent who said it was the nation's most important problem in 1988.[19] This change in public priorities was a clue to perceptive politicians that social rather than economic issues were likely to be more important to the electorate in 1988.

Uncovering matters of concern

Questions that ask for ratings of concern about specified issues and satisfaction with existing government policies can help differentiate issues that are most salient in the public's thinking from those that have a lower priority—for example, "Here is a list of things people have told us they are concerned about today. Would you read over that list and then tell me which two or three you personally are most concerned about today?" Some private pollsters place great weight on questions that measure generalized feelings about the state of the nation—for example, Wirthlin's question, "Is the country moving in the right direction or has it gone off on the wrong track?" Pollsters also often ask whether the respondent would be more likely or less likely to vote for a candidate who takes a given position on an issue—for example, "Would you be more likely to vote for a candidate who favors the death penalty for drug pushers or for a candidate who opposes it?" Still another type of question used by some pollsters asks whether various statements are good or bad arguments for a particular issue position—for example, "I am going to read some arguments that have been given in favor of the death penalty for people who have been convicted of selling drugs. Whether you personally favor or oppose the death penalty, please tell me which, if any, of them you think is a good argument in favor of it?"

Distinguishing effective arguments

Answers to questions like the foregoing help distinguish issues that will influence voting decisions from those that, even though they are important, are unlikely to change votes and can therefore be safely ignored. These responses also alert candidates to their strong suits and their vulnerabilities as well as to those of their opponents. These answers also help a candidate select the most persuasive, as distinct from the most cogent, arguments—an activity that Charles Roll and Albert Cantril have called "positioning an issue."[20] The goal of private pollsters in asking questions such as these is to discover what issues can make a difference politically and how to present those issues, not to help a candidate decide what position to take on them.

Positioning issues

Positioning an issue does not mean that a candidate has to make a commitment to specific legislative programs. Rather, all that a candidate has to do is appear to demonstrate an involvement in the electorate's concerns, with the goal of convincing voters that attention will be paid to those concerns. In his successful 1987 campaign to be elected governor of Mississippi, Ray Mabus relied on exactly that approach:

A month before Mabus announced his candidacy the Washington media consulting firm Doak, Shrum and Associates was already testing the electorate with surveys, which revealed that Mabus's theme of drastic change would hit big—"It just leapt out at you." . . . The campaign was light on specifics but heavy on image, but that was just the point. "You just say 'Imagine what he could do as Governor,' and let the voters decide what he'll do."[21]

Using polls to position issues is quite different from adopting as one's own whatever position polls report to be supported by a majority of voters. Instead, it involves the adoption of a marketing approach to the development of campaign strategy and tactics. When taking a marketing approach, campaign strategists decide how to position an issue on the basis of the persuasiveness of alternative arguments, as determined through an analysis of the electorate's motivations and self-defined needs. The public is polled to discover which problems have high priority and which aspects of those problems are of greatest concern but not to determine how the public wants those problems solved.

The use of polls to select and position issues places a premium on a combination of political experience and analytic expertise. Merely asking questions that measure the split of opinion on an issue will not suffice. In order to develop questions that will tap deep-seated feelings and then analyze the answers in relation to what is politically feasible, the private pollster should have technical training. This furthers the professionalization and bureaucratization of election campaigning. Pressure on private pollsters to become part of a team devoted to the development of effective campaign strategies, rather than serving as an impartial conduit for informing political leaders about the public's wishes, is also increased.

To some degree polls probably sensitize political candidates to the public's needs. At the same time, the stress on issue areas rather than on preferred solutions gives the public a role in establishing political priorities and in setting the public agenda without requiring the public to serve in an expert capacity for which it is unqualified. To the extent that this happens, polls supplement the function of elections as a mechanism for furthering governmental responsibility and responsiveness. Still, relying on professional pollsters for political intelligence does not necessarily result in the adoption of the public's preferences when candidates formulate their policy positions. All that may happen is that candidates for political office will emphasize selected themes that resonate well during a campaign, without any follow-through if elected. In 1986, drug addiction was a major theme in congressional election campaigns, but legislation on this problem did not have high priority in the new Congress, and the Reagan administration actually reduced spending on drug programs. It was not until 1988, in the heat of that year's election campaign, that Congress enacted significant new legislation on drug control.

As is evident from the preceding discussion, analyzing poll results to select and position issues can contribute to the exploitation of issues in order to attract votes to politicians who may not necessarily have programs for coping with those issues. There is nothing new about candidates not keeping promises after they are elected to office. Polling's specific contribution is to enable candidates to tailor their campaign appeals precisely to the public's current worries and fears, leaving the impression that they truly are of a mind with their constituencies. In this way, private polls contribute more to the manipulation of the public than to the meeting of its needs and wants.

Selecting Candidates

The use of polls to decide which candidates to support has probably received the least attention from the general public even though its effects are far-reaching. Faith in the putative predictive power of preelection polls has led to the assumption that early polls are a dependable guide to identifying winners and avoiding losers. As a result, it is now common practice for party committees and major contributors to examine the results of early polls when deciding which aspiring nominee to support.

Politicians and political analysts alike have been impressed by the extent to which the selection of nominees for elective office and the ability to raise money are determined by poll standings. Roll and Cantril reported that early polls have a major effect on the ability of lesser known candidates to stay in a race.[22] Nathan Glazer and Daniel Patrick Moynihan relate how the 1962 nomination of Robert M. Morgenthau as the Democratic candidate for governor of New York was strongly influenced by poll results that were interpreted to indicate that a qualified Jewish candidate had the best chance of defeating Nelson Rockefeller.[23] In 1968, *Time* quoted Richard Nixon as saying, "When the polls go good for me, the cash register really rings."[24] Hubert Humphrey's difficulty in raising funds in that same year's presidential campaign has been commonly ascribed to his abysmally poor showing in early polls.

Potential candidates as well as potential supporters often rely on early polls when deciding whether to run for office. Rudolph Giuliani reportedly decided not to seek nomination as the Republican candidate for senator in New York's 1988 election because polls conducted in 1987 documented the apparently insuperable strength of Patrick Moynihan, the Democratic incumbent.[25] Vermont's governor Madeline M. Kunin, when announcing that she would seek a third term in 1988 instead of running for U.S. senator, revealed that a poll she had commissioned had showed her trailing the announced Republican candidate for senator.[26]

In its role of winnowing out potential aspirants to office, belief in the predictive accuracy of poll standings has acted to narrow the choice of candidates presented to the public for its consideration. In this way, early poll standings define for politicians and contributors, and also the news media, who is electable and therefore worthy of attention and who is not. As a result, voting inclinations as they exist *before* election campaigns start gain undue weight. As we shall discuss later, this reliance on early polls is based on a misconception of their meaning, which is why expectations based on early polls often prove wrong. Nonetheless, by narrowing the choices presented to the public for its consideration and by creating an additional barrier for aspiring newcomers who start from positions of early weakness, polls have significantly influenced the process through which the choices made available to the electorate are determined.

Although there can be no question regarding the significant impact that polls have had upon the nominating process and upon the ability of aspirants to office to attract financial support, polls are not all determining in these respects. If Hubert Humphrey's fundraising in 1968 was crippled by his poor standing in the polls, Barry Goldwater ended his 1964 campaign with a sizable surplus despite his dreadful performance in that year's preelection polls. Humphrey's resurgence in the final weeks of the 1968 campaign was due at least in part to the fact that the AFL-CIO, made fearful by polls showing an across-the-board Democratic debacle, launched a vigorous drive on Humphrey's behalf during the final weeks before election. Jimmy Carter, a complete unknown in polls conducted in the beginning of 1976, moved to a commanding position by the time the Democratic Convention met in July of that year. In contrast, Edward Kennedy's bid to be the Democratic nominee for president went nowhere in 1980, despite what appeared to be a commanding position in early polls. In 1987, Gary Hart registered strong pubic support in polls conducted immediately after his reentry into the preprimary campaign, only to fail miserably in all the 1988 primaries and caucuses in which he actually ran. The dynamics of election campaigns are too complex to be reduced to a matter of who is ahead in early polls.

POLLS AND POLICYMAKING

Although polls play a major role in the conduct of election campaigns, we cannot automatically conclude that they also play a major role in policymaking. We must determine whether opinion polls influence policy decisions between elections or influence decisions made by nonelected officials in the executive branch as well as by elected officials.

Polls regarding public policy issues are conducted for a variety of sponsors, with diverse interests and purposes. Best known are media-sponsored polls, but surveys sponsored by government agencies, special interest groups, and corporations must also be considered. Furthermore, we must consider the attention paid to polls by policymakers who do not, themselves, sponsor them.

The Role of Media-Sponsored Polls

Some media-sponsored polls, such as the ABC News/*Washington Post* Poll, the CBS News/*New York Times* Poll, and the NBC News/*Wall Street Journal* Poll, are conducted by the media themselves using in-house resources. Others, such as the Gallup, Harris, and California Polls, are conducted by commercial survey organizations and are then syndicated to media subscribers. *USA Today* uses Gordon Black to conduct its polls, and still others, such as the Minnesota Poll, are designed by the news organization and are then conducted by outside survey research firms. In all cases, media-sponsored polls must be designed to meet journalistic needs as well as criteria of sound survey methodology.[27]

Professional notions of objectivity, newsworthiness, and timeliness, rather than partisan or special interest group concerns, determine the selection of topics and question wordings. The intent of media-sponsored polls is to report the news—in this case, the news about public opinion. (Conceptions of what is "news" and how these conceptions influence polling are discussed in Chapter 4.) While specific questions asked in media-sponsored polls may be criticized as faulty or biased, the professional credo of objective reporting governs the environment within which they are conducted and reported. This contrasts with those polls (to be discussed later) that are commissioned with the express intention of furthering a special interest. The presumed objectivity of media-sponsored polls, plus the fact that they are virtually guaranteed prominent public exposure, gives them a potential for considerable political impact. This potential, however, is seldom realized with respect to policy decisionmaking.

Because newsworthiness and timeliness must always be taken into account when selecting topics for media polls, the intrinsic significance of an issue is often a secondary consideration. Polls on Social Security became common only after the financial health of the program reached crisis proportions, not during the preceding years when experts were becoming concerned about the impending crisis.[28] Terrorist attacks can trigger a temporary surge of polls on that issue, as can the drug-induced death of a prominent athlete, the decision of liability insurance companies to deal with their financial problems by drastically increasing premiums, the staging of a rock concert to raise money for starving Ethiopians, or a nationwide demonstration for a nuclear freeze. Policymakers, who must operate in a time perspective of years, cannot be expected to make much use of polls guided by such headline priorities.

The limited amount of time or space available for reporting also severely restricts the news media in conducting in-depth investigations of public opinion. Because poll results will usually be compressed into a short report, typically only two or three questions are asked on any one issue. The results of such polls cannot provide much guidance to policymakers.

The preoccupation of media-sponsored polls with newsworthiness and timeliness, in conjunction with the practice of asking only a few questions on any one issue, acts to preclude any continuing, in-depth effort to report how public opinion emerges and takes shape with respect to fundamental issues facing the country. The consequence is an often superficial and stuttering picture of public thinking on issues. (On the other hand, until the public's attention is focused on an issue by major events, much of the public will be ill-informed and even unaware of it and therefore without an opinion about it.) In any event, policymakers cannot usually get much guidance regarding the public's desires and preferences from media-sponsored polls. Only occasionally, when an editorial decision is made to base a major feature story on poll results, is there any possibility that media-sponsored polls will probe the complexities of public opinion in a way that will give policymakers usable information.

The Role of Government Surveys

The many surveys conducted for government agencies and officials who make public policy[29] might seem good sources for learning about public opinion, but in fact they are not. Typically, these surveys are factfinding projects—for example, surveying patterns of food consumption, commuting to work, or health care behavior—and not polls on the public's opinion on issues. Many of these surveys are *need assessments* designed to collect "objective" facts that can be used to determine whether there is a definable need for a program. Others are *evaluation* studies that seek to assess how successful a program has been. Often, attitudes and opinions are not measured at all. Even when they are, they act simply as an aid to the implementation of a program rather than as a guide to policymaking.

Polling to aid policy implementation

A study I conducted for the National Highway Traffic Safety Administration (NHTSA) illustrates the distinction between polling to set policy and polling to further an already determined policy. The study tested the acceptability of a number of highway safety countermeasures that NHTSA was considering. Concerned that some of the measures under consideration would meet with adamant public resistance, which would endanger the entire program, NHTSA sought to discover which measures would be accepted by the public and which would not. Similar in some ways to polls of public opinion, this study differed in that the results were used to make the implementation of existing policy more effective, not to set policy. This survey resembled marketing research more than public opinion polling.

The parallel between marketing research and governmental agency surveys is very close. When public cooperation is essential to the successful implementation of a program, government agencies are relatively likely to survey public attitudes and feelings. For example, the Internal Revenue Service (IRS) has for some time conducted surveys designed to help it get better cooperation from taxpayers and to reduce cheating. Some of those studies have tested reactions to reporting forms and instructions for filling them out so as reduce problems generated by the complexity of tax forms. For that purpose, questions that might be asked include, "Which of these two forms do you prefer for attractiveness? simplicity of instructions? How much help will you need to fill it out?" Other IRS studies have investigated motivations for cheating and the characteristics of cheaters so as to develop more effective ways of dealing with that problem. Those surveys ask questions such as, "What do you think is the main thing that keeps people from cheating?" "Do you think the chances that a tax return will be audited are increased if the person claims certain kinds of expenses, exemptions, or deductions?" "Suppose you knew someone was cheating on his income tax. Would you write the government about it, or do nothing about it, or what?" But studies such as these are very different from public opinion polls conducted to determine what tax policy should be. There is a very important distinction between asking the foregoing questions versus asking, "Do you favor or oppose decreasing the capital gains tax?"

The parallel between some government-sponsored polls and marketing research is not necessarily pejorative. When government-sponsored polls deal with policies whose effectiveness depends upon the public's voluntary compliance, these polls can sensitize government agencies to public attitudes and motivations that might otherwise be overlooked. To the extent that this happens, the use of polls by government agencies introduces a modicum of the quasidemocracy of the marketplace to government by bureaucracy. Even when the express purpose of a study is to further an already formulated policy, an occasional unintended consequence is to modify policies so that they conform more closely to the public's desires than would otherwise be the case. A study commissioned by New York City's Metropolitan Transportation Authority (MTA) illustrates how this might happen.

The MTA had hoped that the study would suggest ways to encourage car drivers to use commuter trains, subways, and buses.[30] Instead, the study showed that the assumptions underlying existing policies were flawed and that if large numbers of car drivers were to be converted into mass transit passengers, new strategies would have to be developed. The study concluded that because of an unanticipated flourishing "car culture," many car drivers "would never consider public transportation regardless of the quality of improvements made." Even those car drivers who might consider mass transit felt that the many logistical barriers they would encounter when using public transportation made it unattractive. Official reaction at the MTA was one of discouragement, and further research was planned.

Polling to aid program planning

Polls can also be very useful to government agencies in planning informational and outreach programs by defining the public's awareness and understanding of social problems. One such poll, conducted by the Center for Work Performance Problems at the Georgia Institute of Technology, found that a large segment of the labor force feared working alongside AIDS sufferers. In discussing the implications of this finding, David M. Herold stressed that employers had to educate their work forces that casual contact does not spread AIDS: "If people are catatonic because they have a co-worker with AIDS, the impact on productivity and efficiency is going to be great."[31]

Gallup's original conception of the role of public opinion polls was almost implemented by a survey that the Social Security Administration (SSA) contemplated conducting in 1979. At the time debate as to whether the financial structure of the Social Security system might have to be changed had attracted the general public's attention. The survey was to poll public attitudes regarding alternative methods of financing Social Security. Initially, SSA authorized Mathematica Policy Research to conduct a pilot survey (of which I was principal co-investigator) on how to design such a survey. The proposed poll was unusual in that it was intended to provide information about which of several courses of action the public preferred and was to aid the drafting of new legislation. The project never got past the development of a draft questionnaire and two years later, in 1981, was canceled. Eventually, the Reagan administration and the Congress agreed to have a special commission study the problem and make its legislative recommendations. That commission relied on the traditional practice of having witnesses from various special interest groups provide input from "the public."

Polling to support existing policies

When a government agency does commission a public opinion poll, there is a strong likelihood that the results will be interpreted by the agency to support policies already in place. A 1988 poll conducted by Rutgers University's Eagleton Institute for the New Jersey Department of Transportation illustrates this pattern. As reported by the *Newark Star-Ledger,* this poll showed that "a growing number of New Jersey residents believe the state's quality of life will deteriorate during the next decade and more than half feel the pace of development has sped out of control."[32] At the time the poll was conducted, the state legislature was considering a package of bills, proposed by the Department of Transportation, that would give the department and individual counties new regulatory power over land development.

Transportation Commissioner Hazel Gluck concluded from the poll that the proposed legislation's stated goal of achieving a balance between environmental control and economic development was vindicated. Noting that the poll revealed a rather even split between pro- and no-growth adherents, she added that "to prevent the balance tipping toward anti-growth forces, the development community must accept new regulatory controls to assure future growth takes place in a more orderly environment."[33] Countering that conclusion, Patrick O'Keefe, vice president of the New Jersey Builders Association, asserted that a poll his organization had commissioned the previous year revealed that a majority of New Jersey residents wanted more affordable housing.[34] Regardless of the merit of the proposed legislation and without questioning the validity of the Rutgers poll (its methodological credentials appear impeccable), it is clear that the poll was used to justify policy rather than to help formulate it.

Polling to gain public input

An infrequent but potentially productive use of polls by legislative bodies is to have pollsters report in committee hearings on the results of the many polls they have conducted. For example, in October 1975, as a way of getting "public input" into its investigation of the state of the national economy, the Joint Economic Committee of the Congress of the United States asked for testimony from the Conference Board (a private sector organization that conducts periodic surveys on consumer confidence and corporate planning), the Gallup Poll, and the Harris Survey. Results of polls on the public's economic concerns and buying plans were reported to the committee by, respectively, Fabian Linden, myself, and Louis Harris. Archives of polling organizations are a nonpartisan resource for information about public opinion that is readily available to legislatures but is seldom utilized.

Government monitoring of polls

In addition to sponsoring polls, some government agencies, such as the State Department, have active programs for monitoring public opinion polls.[35] The Congressional Research Office of the Library of Congress maintains a clipping file of polls that is available to senators and representatives for their information. But, typically, government monitoring of polls is done to identify the extent and nature of public support for existing or proposed policies, not to formulate policy. For instance, Franklin Roosevelt, who pioneered the use of polls for monitoring public support, relied on polls to track public reaction to his policy of providing Lend-Lease aid to Great Britain before the United States entered World War II.[36] Those polls showed that even though the volume of aid was increasing, the percentages of the electorate that felt Roosevelt was going too far, about right, or not far enough remained constant all through 1941. That increasing aid was not generating rising opposition reassured Roosevelt that it was politically safe to continue that policy, not that he *should* continue it.

In describing the State Department's more recent monitoring activities, Bernard Roshco commented that

> polls could not tell policy makers whether the interests of the United States would be well-served by a treaty drastically revising the provisions for control and maintenance of the Panama Canal. But the polls did tell policy makers that the public saw no need for such a treaty and was not even acquainted with the concerns that had induced successive administrations, both Democratic and Republican, to continue a painstaking negotiation. That the Panama Canal Treaties were barely ratified after a prolonged debate and last-minute modification is the case in point.[37]

Implicit in Roshco's comment is the belief that if the Carter administration had paid close attention to poll reports on the public's opinion about the Panama Canal Treaties, it might have dealt more effectively with the intense opposition the treaties encountered in the Senate. He admonished policymakers that "if those responsible for making and changing policy want to increase the likelihood that their proposals will be adopted, they would be well-advised to become sophisticated readers of poll findings."[38] In other words, the importance for policymakers that Roshco ascribes to polls is their utility for promoting policy, not for making it.

In the same vein, James Fallows, drawing upon his experience on the White House staff in the Carter administration, reported, "The polling data I usually saw in the government were connected with the *salesmanship* of a program, as opposed to the development of its policy."[39] Paul Warnke, chief U.S. negotiator at the Strategic Arms Limitation Talks (SALT), expressed a similar attitude in his description of how policymakers use public opinion polls:

> On SALT, with its [the poll's] effect on substance, I think it is pretty clear that polls can't affect the substance. . . . You can't conduct a negotiation by referendum. . . . It's hard enough, as a negotiator, to conduct it with the restraints put on you by the Washington bureaucracy. And if you try to deal with polls too, I think you'd get no place at all. . . . The effect of polls on SALT has to do more with the tactics of presentation of the case for SALT than it ever could with the substance of SALT.[40]

When it comes to the formation of policy, the standard response of policymaking officials to poll results is, according to Roshco, "They can't be useful, since the public doesn't understand the complexity of our problems."[41] Adam Yarmolinsky expressed an even more negative view that discounted the relevance of any measures of public opinion to the real tasks involved in policymaking: "There are surprisingly few operationally significant questions for the policy maker as to which any public opinion, in my view, exists. By an operationally significant question, I mean a question the answer to which will affect specific actions of government officials. The overwhelming bulk of those questions are of means and not of ends."[42] Susan King, during her tenure as chairperson of the Consumer Product Safety Commission, remarked, "Polls are not useful to us . . . in terms of offering much in the way of policy guidance. That is, they do not tell regulators *what* it is we should be doing, because we operate under rather well-defined statutes. What we are to do is quite clear: It's set down in the law."[43] Clearly, the dominant view among appointed members of the executive branch is that although polls may in some circumstances be tactically useful for selling a program, they are irrelevant in defining an agency's mission and in spelling out rules and regulations, except when the public's cooperation is needed to implement a program.

The Role of Polls in Influencing Elected Officeholders

The responsiveness of elected officeholders to public opinion polls when formulating their policy goals must be considered separately from the responsiveness of government agencies and appointed officials because elected officials have a different relationship with the public. Because elected officials must seek reelection to remain in office, they cannot avoid listening to their constituencies. But even if elected officials listen through polls, they do not necessarily automatically conform to the public's wishes as registered in polls.

One good way of evaluating the responsiveness of elected officials to poll results is to compare poll results on issues with the policies of the Reagan administration. Some of the differences that emerge are startling, especially in light of Reagan's success in maintaining high popularity through most of his two terms of office. A few illustrations from polls taken during 1985–1986, a period when Reagan's ratings in the polls were uniformly high, should suffice.

In regard to military spending (Reagan policy was to increase military spending):

- A **June 1985** ABC News/*Washington Post* poll reported that by a margin of 56 percent to 38 percent, a majority felt that "the government is spending too much money on the military." That same poll also found that by a margin of 57 percent to 41 percent, the majority agreed that the government should "make substantial cuts in military spending to reduce the budget."[44]
- A **February 1986** Gallup Poll reported that 59 percent of those polled approved cuts in defense spending as a way of reducing the federal budget deficit.[45]
- In **March 1986,** the Gallup Poll reported that 47 percent believed the United States was spending too much "for national defense and military purposes," 13 percent believed the amount was too little, and 36 percent believed the amount was about right.[46]

In regard to spending on domestic programs (Reagan charged domestic spending was excessive):

- A **June 1985** ABC News/*Washington Post* poll found that by a margin of 59 percent to 39 percent, the majority opposed "substantial cuts in spending for social programs to reduce the budget deficit." In that same poll, by a margin of 56 percent to 37 percent, the majority disagreed with the statement that "the government is spending too much tax money on social programs."[47]

- In a **January 1986** CBS News/*New York Times* poll, 39 percent thought that government programs in the 1960s designed to help the poor generally made things better, compared with 18 percent who thought those programs made things worse. Another 38 percent thought those programs did not have much impact. Moreover, a majority of 66 percent agreed that the government "should spend money now on a similar effort to try to improve the conditions of poor people in this country," whereas 22 percent opposed such a spending effort.[48]

- A **February 1986** CBS News/*New York Times* poll reported 50 percent in favor of increasing spending on programs such as price supports, grants, and loans to help farmers, 12 percent who wanted such spending decreased, and 30 percent who felt spending should be kept at its current level.[49]

- A **February 1986** Gallup Poll found a minority of 42 percent in favor of cutting spending on social programs in order to reduce the federal budget deficit.[50]

On Nicaragua (Reagan policy was to provide military support to the contra opposition to the Sandinista government):

- In **June 1985,** the ABC News/*Washington Post* poll found that by a majority of 71 percent to 18 percent, the public felt that the United States should *not* be involved in trying to overthrow the government in Nicaragua.[51]

- A **March 1986** Gallup Poll reported that by a margin of 52 percent to 35 percent the public felt that Congress should *not* authorize a "new aid package . . . of $100,000,000 to the rebels seeking to overthrow the communist government in Nicaragua."[52]

- An **April 1986** CBS News/*New York Times* poll reported that by a margin of 62 percent to 25 percent, the public opposed giving "$100 million in military and other aid to the contras trying to overthrow the government in Nicaragua."[53]

Polls on nuclear testing and Reagan's Strategic Defense Initiative (Star Wars) showed a more complex pattern of public thinking, but in this case as well there was a considerable gap between public opinion and Reagan's policies:

- A **July 1985** ABC News/*Washington Post* poll reported majority disapproval of plans to develop a space-based defense weapons plan, by a margin of 53 percent to 41 percent.[54]
- In contrast, a **November 1985** *Los Angeles Times* poll found that by a margin of 58 percent to 30 percent, the majority felt the United States "should undertake a Strategic Defense Initiative." But in that same poll, only a minority believed that such a program would be effective: 10 percent thought it would provide a "leakproof umbrella," and another 32 percent believed it would reduce the number of missiles that would get through.[55]
- In **June 1986,** the Gallup Poll found that by 56 percent to 35 percent, a majority felt that the United States should agree "to a ban on nuclear testing if the Soviet Union continues their ban."[56]

The questions asked in the preceding polls by no means probed all dimensions of public opinion on the issues involved, and there were other important issues on which majorities agreed with Reagan administration policies. Nonetheless, the cited polls clearly indicated that much of the public, in some cases a decided majority, opposed the basic thrust of policies that had been vigorously pushed by a president they reelected in overwhelming numbers. To explain this seeming paradox would take a separate, complex analysis, but we can say indisputably that elected officeholders can and do act in the face of public opinion polls when making policy decisions. Moreover, a politician who does not follow the polls when making policy decisions is not automatically doomed to failure. On the contrary, skillful politicians such as Ronald Reagan can achieve the highest pinnacles of success even when they campaign vigorously for policies that, judging from polls, the public opposes.

Some elected government officials authorize polls through private channels in a manner similar to the permanent campaign style of governing described previously and not as part of an agency's policymaking activities. Such polls are often *trial balloons* that test public concern about an issue and receptivity to proposed legislation dealing with it. For example, Nelson Rockefeller, when governor of New York, commissioned private polls that tested whether the public would respond favorably to proposed legislation on such issues as crime and narcotics. However, these polls were designed not so much to get policy ideas from the public as to determine the political appeal of the issues.[57]

Legislative bodies rarely commission polls specifically to learn the public's views on issues, but Harris did conduct a poll in 1975 on public confidence in government for the Senate Committee on Government Operations. Significantly, that survey was part of a bipartisan effort to investigate the sources of declining confidence in government. Because of the bipartisan sponsorship, the results of that poll were spared the otherwise-to-be-expected charge that they were rigged to further the interests of one party or faction.

When making policy decisions, elected government officials are sensitive to public opinion polls in the packaging of the policy but not in the determination of policy content. There is no evidence that public opinion polls have become a decisive factor in the formation of public policy, as the early pollsters hoped and the early critics feared. Instead, polls function primarily as political intelligence for politicians as they develop election campaign strategies and attempt to sell the public on policies that have already been decided.

The Role of Nongovernment Polls

For a complete analysis of the role public opinion polls actually play in our political life, we must also consider polls commissioned by a variety of private, nongovernmental groups. Some of these polls are conducted to further the interests and goals of special interest groups, while others are, at least ostensibly, conducted in the public interest.

Special-interest-group polls

Special interest groups that typically sponsor polls include trade associations, volunteer public service organizations, individual corporations, and political action groups. The subject matter of these polls is as diverse as the groups that commission them: nuclear disarmament, abortion, education, government regulation of hazardous materials, tax legislation, environmental concerns, child care, health care, problems of the aged. Whatever the issue, these polls are conducted to identify the public's preconceptions about the issues involved and how knowledgeable, or ignorant, the public is about those issues. Aspirations, fears, and values that predispose the public favorably or unfavorably to various courses of action are also identified through such polls.

When special interest groups commission polls of public opinion, they do so for two distinctly different reasons. (1) Frequently, such polls are intended for in-house use only to help plan lobbying, advertising, public outreach, and other communications activities. Because the results of these polls are highly confidential, it is difficult to document them and their frequency. But they are widespread, and all major commercial polling organizations have at some time or other conducted such polls. (2) Many polls are commissioned so that the results can be publicized in a way that will further the interest group's ends. When conducted by trade associations and political action groups, these polls—usually called *advocacy polls*—are used specifically as a means to achieve a predetermined end. When conducted by philanthropic and other public service organizations, they are more likely to be comparable to academic studies and media-sponsored public opinion polls.

Polls for in-house use. Polls for in-house use are normally used to determine how to present the sponsoring group's position most effectively to the public, not to decide the sponsor's position. Another in-house use is to monitor public opinion in order to evaluate how effective the sponsor's communications have been and to determine the need for further action. A less common in-house use of polls is to assess the organization's activities—for example, how to improve fundraising activities or recruitment of volunteers. These applications illustrate how private groups use polls to gain information that can help develop effective lobbying and public relations rather than to decide what public policy should be.

Although the results of polls commissioned for in-house use by special interest groups are not intended to be disseminated to the public, when these results appear to support the position of the sponsoring group, selected results are occasionally released. When this happens, a common practice is to release only favorable results. This, of course, may create a distorted picture of the public's thinking on the issue, even if the released results are factually correct.

Advocacy polls. Special interest groups also commission polls in order to release the results, sometimes in a controlled manner only to legislators and sometimes to the general public. But as with results of polls originally intended for in-house use only, release of advocacy polls is contingent on whether the results support the position of the sponsoring group. If the poll's results are negative, they are usually suppressed (although, on occasion, some negative results are released in order to enhance the poll's credibility as an objective investigation). Sometimes, to assure that a poll's results will be beneficial to the sponsor's purposes, a small-scale *pilot* study may be conducted to identify those questions that will produce favorable answers. The full-scale poll will ask only those questions; then the results of the full-scale poll can be "safely" released.

When the results of advocacy polls are shown only to legislators, the purpose is to persuade them that there are political gains to be made, or at least no risk to be incurred, in adopting the position that favors the interests of lobbyist clients. An example of a poll intended primarily for presentation to legislative bodies is one I directed when I was with The Gallup Organization. The poll was conducted for American Express at a time when Congress was considering legislation that would deregulate airline fares. The poll investigated in considerable depth the attitudes and preferences of air travelers regarding air fares and services. (I designed the poll and its analysis, and I wrote the report. It was agreed beforehand that the report would be released in its entirety.) Its results were presented by American Express to members of Congress in support of. its position that existing regulations and practices were not serving the public's desires. The report's influence on the deregulatory legislation that was enacted is difficult to assess, but American Express obviously thought it would be influential.

When advocacy poll results are released to the general public, the intent is also to influence legislators, but through the agency of the general public. The New York City Real Estate Board sponsored a typical advocacy poll intended for public release. The president of the board, Steven Spinola, said the purpose of the poll was to determine if there was growing antidevelopment feeling in the city. The poll was reported by the board to have found "a reservoir of support among residents for commercial and residential development."[58]

Two examples of advocacy polls that were released to the general public show that legislators do not necessarily tailor their voting to fit majority opinion as measured in polls. During the debate on the Equal Rights Amendment, proponents repeatedly cited polls that indicated majority support for its adoption. Similarly, proponents of the legalized right to abortion, such as Planned Parenthood, have repeatedly cited polls (some sponsored by them and some by the news media) showing majority support for their position. In both these instances, however, the release of opinion poll results has had, at best, limited political success. In these instances, the effect of public release of advocacy polls has been not so much to determine policy decisions as to increase the attention paid to public opinion during public debates of controversial issues.

Given that advocacy polls are released only when their results favor the sponsoring organization's position, even if a given poll stands up to professional scrutiny, advocacy polls as such cannot be automatically relied on to provide an objective picture of public opinion. Their avowed intent is to influence policymakers by claiming that the public wants the course of action espoused by the sponsoring group to be adopted. The credibility of such polls is always suspect because this intent is always apparent. For this reason, special interest groups typically engage the services of well-known, respected polling firms that are unlikely to endanger their reputations, and their business, by conducting obviously biased polls. (Review of the research design and questionnaire by an independent, presumably objective, organization before the poll is conducted is one procedure for achieving credibility that is sometimes used by the research firm and the sponsoring organization.) Indicative of the ever present need to protect the credibility of advocacy polls, David Schoen, a partner of the polling firm Penn & Schoen that conducted the New York Real Estate Board poll mentioned previously, was quoted in the *New York Times* as saying that the poll's questions were formulated by his firm, not by members or employees of the Real Estate Board.[59]

A personal experience I had when I was with The Gallup Organization exemplifies the ethical issues encountered by polling organizations when they conduct advocacy polls. I was contacted by a major national corporation that was planning to commission a study on consumer attitudes regarding interest rate charges on indebtedness. The intent was to show to key legislators only poll results that favored the corporation's position. But Gallup policy was that the corporation had to commit itself in advance to release the entire report, favorable or unfavorable, or else not release the report at all. This condition was not acceptable to the corporation, and Gallup was not commissioned to conduct the poll.

A particularly controversial use of advocacy polls is described by Bogart.[60] In 1969, during a bitter Senate debate on the Safeguard antiballistic missile (ABM) system, a group that favored installing the system placed a full-page advertisement in leading newspapers with the headline "84% of All Americans Support an ABM System." As it turned out, the advertisement did not report all the poll results and concealed significant aspects of the questions asked on the poll. Eventually, after a number of prominent opinion research practitioners protested publicly, Opinion Research Corporation, the organization that had conducted the poll, repudiated its use in the advertisement.

The Role of Public-Service-Group Polls

The final category of polls for us to consider are those sponsored by groups that have no apparent axe to grind. Two very dissimilar types of organizations are sponsors of these polls.

Public service groups

Public service groups such as the Chicago Council on Foreign Relations, the Charles Kettering Foundation, and the Public Agenda Foundation have sponsored major studies of public opinion on such issues as U.S. foreign policy, the adequacy of the nation's educational institutions, and attitudes regarding employment and work. These studies have investigated underlying beliefs, concerns, and feelings about issues and have not been restricted to the specifics of legislative proposals.

Because of the depth of investigation, these polls can provide a nonpartisan insight into public opinion on politically sensitive issues that is difficult to derive from media-sponsored polls. The express intent of these public service polls is to inform policymakers about the "hopes and fears of the American people," to borrow the title from the report on one such study.[61] The expectation is that such information will help policymakers do a better job of addressing the issues of concern to the public, not that policymakers will use the results to determine what that policy should be. Potomac Associates, sponsor of a number of major surveys of public opinion, identified its purpose as "encouraging lively inquiry into critical issues of public policy. . . . to heighten public understanding and improve public discourse on significant contemporary problems."[62] The credibility of these polls is presumably assured by their nonpartisan sponsorship and the credentials of the organizations that conduct them, although this does not protect them from attack by groups that disagree with the thrust of the poll results. However controversial their results may become, these polls add a dimension to public debate that would otherwise be missing.

An indication of the influence polls sponsored by public service organization can have are the annual Gallup polls on public attitudes regarding education originally funded by the Charles Kettering Foundation in 1969 and still sponsored by Phi Delta Kappa.[63] The results of these polls are published each year in *Phi Delta Kappan* and the *Gallup Report* and are widely reported in newspapers and public service television programs. Educational leaders have come to rely on the results of these polls when assessing public opinion regarding the performance of the nation's schools. This is an unusual instance, however, and the irregularity and infrequency with which most public service polls are conducted limit their potential significance.

Mention should also be made of polls conducted for nonpartisan public service groups that nonetheless find themselves enmeshed in public controversy. I directed such a poll in 1973—on public knowledge of and attitudes toward the diagnosis and treatment of breast cancer— on behalf of the American Cancer Society. Included in the poll, which was conducted at a time when the society's policy of recommending radical mastectomy was being criticized by some groups, were questions intended to cast light on why many women did not use available diagnostic techniques and surgical treatments. The results were presented at a press conference that emphasized, among other things, the pressing need to educate women about effective means for diagnosing and treating breast cancer.

Corporate sponsors

Major studies of public opinion have been sponsored by corporations on topics that have no direct, substantive relation to their business. The motive for conducting these studies is that they have public relations value for the sponsoring corporations. Illustrative are the periodic surveys of U.S. women sponsored by Virginia Slims, the series of General Mills studies on the U.S. family, and the Connecticut Mutual Life study, "Values in the 1980s." These polls tend to avoid partisan issues, and the disinterested nature of their sponsorship gives them credibility. Also, they often probe opinion on social trends in considerable depth. However, their obvious public relations function often limits the attention they receive.

Nevertheless, when the results of such polls are relevant to controversial public issues, they may get the attention of the news media. Thus, the report, "The American Teacher 1988: Strengthening the Relationship Between Teachers and Students," commissioned by the Metropolitan Life Insurance Company and conducted by Louis Harris & Associates, was the basis for a four-column news story on the education page of the *New York Times*[64] Although the poll covered a number of topics, the *Times* headlined the fact that a sizable proportion of teachers were planning to quit their profession (26 percent) and that this intention was particularly common among minority teachers. More typically, news releases on such polls seldom merit more than a short paragraph.

POLLS IN AUTHORITARIAN SOCIETIES

The adoption of polling in the People's Republic of China under Deng Xiaoping's leadership gives us an instructive perspective on the use of public opinion polls in the United States. Wu Xin, head of survey operations at the National Research Center for Science and Technology for Development, explained the rise of polling in China as necessitated by economic reforms: "Recently the Government has paid a lot of attention to surveys. During China's reforms, the economic system has changed a lot. The Government wants to know if the mass of people will go along with it. If the policy proceeds too rapidly, or the methods aren't right and the people are opposed to it, it will fail."[65] Edward A. Gargan, the *New York Times* reporter who interviewed Wu, further observed that "in a country more comfortable with unanimity than pluralism, his [Wu's] efforts represent a profound shift in the Government's long held assumption that it invariably makes the correct decision."[66] As the Chinese economy was modified to allow more room for individual initiative, successful governing became more dependent on the political leadership being informed about public response to those modifications, and polls were adopted as an effective means for becoming informed. That is to say, the purpose of polling in China is to enable the still totalitarian government to pursue its goals more effectively. We should not conclude that the use of polls presages a conversion of the People's Republic of China into a Western-style democracy.

In the Soviet Union, along with the liberalizing policies of *glasnost'* (openness) and *perestroika* (restructuring) instituted by Mikhail Gorbachev, polls have become an acceptable information-gathering technique. An unusual manifestation of this development are polls developed cooperatively by Soviet and U.S. news organizations. In one case, a poll of Moscow residents was commissioned by the *New York Times* and conducted by the Institute for Sociological Research of the Soviet Academy of Sciences. The *Times* paid the institute to conduct the survey, the *Times* Moscow Bureau submitted the topic, and its director of news surveys (Michael Kagay) wrote the questionnaire.[67] *Newsweek* and Novosti (a Soviet news service) commissioned a poll that involved interviewing in both the United States and the Soviet Union. The Gallup Organization conducted the U.S. phase, and the Center for the Study of Public Opinion at the Institute for Sociological Research conducted the Soviet phase. The questionnaire was the joint product of Gallup and the institute. Each news organization issued its independent report on the results of the two polls.

Of direct relevance to our concerns are two reasons offered by the Soviet participants to explain their interest in conducting these polls. First, they felt that polls would provide their leadership with more accurate information about the opinions of the Soviet populace than was being obtained through the traditional channel of local functionaries of the Communist party. Second, the Soviet cosponsors believed that the polls would provide an opportunity to present the Soviet people to other nations, especially the United States, in a different and more positive light.[68] But receptiveness to poll results quickly wanes when they do not conform to government policy. Gorbachev is reported to have denounced a poll, "angrily shaking his finger, demanded to be reminded who had published data from a purported public opinion poll that showed little support for his programs . . . [and said it] was unscientific and misleading."[69] In totalitarian as well as democratic nations, polls serve the function of providing political leaders with political intelligence that can be used for manipulative purposes without necessarily increasing a government's responsiveness to public opinion. In this manner, the political intelligence available from polls may be used to subvert rather than respond to public opinion.[70]

CONCLUSION

Despite the bitter controversy generated by the ambitious claims of early pollsters, public opinion polls have not had much effect on top-level policymakers insofar as setting policy is concerned. The significance of polls has been largely restricted to how elections are conducted and how policies are sold to the public. In the executive branch of government polls are occasionally used to help in administering and evaluating programs, but rarely, if ever, to help design programs in accord with public opinion.

The greatest effect of polls has been in the transformation of election campaigns into a managed process of mass communications. This transformation has in some ways sensitized elected officials to public concerns and aspirations, but it has also facilitated a manipulative attitude toward the public among those same officials. Polls are also commonly used by advocacy groups when developing their strategies to influence public opinion. Polls have become a widely used information-gathering technology that have contributed significantly to the effectiveness of those who seek to manipulate the public. What does not appear to have happened is the acceptance by policymakers of polls as a mandate from the people.

3

THE METHODOLOGY
AND MEANING OF POLLS

If the polling method is not correctly understood and applied, it cannot provide us with valid information about public opinion. Consequently, we must clear away the underbrush of misinformation and ignorance about the methodological underpinnings of polling if we are to discover how polls can be made socially useful. Our purpose is not to instruct on how to conduct valid polls; there is an extensive methodological literature on survey research and polling that should be studied by those who intend to conduct polls.[1] We also want to go beyond the efforts of Herbert Asher and Norman Bradburn and Seymour Sudman to give layperson guidelines for interpreting polls correctly.[2] Our purpose is to clarify some basic methodological precepts as a means of identifying how polls must be designed and analyzed if they are to measure public opinion in a meaningful sense.

One reason opinion polls are so misunderstood is that conducting them seems deceptively simple. Most anyone can draw up a list of questions, ask them of a number of people, and then tally the answers. But conducting, analyzing, and interpreting a valid poll are technically demanding skills that draw upon a combination of statistics, social psychology, and political science, plus a good knowledge of everyday politics and current events and a lot of hands-on practical experience.

The following discussion evaluates current polling practices from this perspective.

THE PREDICTIVE ACCURACY
OF PREELECTION POLLS

Because the view that polls can be relied on to predict elections accurately has shaped the way most politicians and members of the general public read all poll results, we start our discussion of poll methodology by focusing on preelection polls. We have seen that the initial acceptance of public opinion polls as a credible source of information about public opinion rested primarily on the belief that preelection polls predict elections accurately. We have also seen that the failure of polls to forecast Truman's reelection in 1948 resulted in a temporary decline in the public's acceptance of polls. Ironically, the Gallup Poll's estimate of the percentage of the popular vote that Truman would receive was closer to the actual vote than its estimate of Roosevelt's vote in 1936. The difference was that in 1936 Gallup correctly "called the winner," whereas in 1948 he did not.

To a considerable degree, the belief that preelection polls are accurate predictors persists. There are three components to this belief, each of which has to be critically examined: (1) the assumption that, with a few notorious exceptions, preelection polls have generally been very accurate, (2) the assumption that preelection polls predict how people will vote, and (3) the assumption that measuring likely voting behavior is comparable to measuring opinions on issues. In fact, each of these assumptions is flawed to some degree, which is one very important reason opinion poll results are so often misinterpreted and misused.

The reputation for accuracy that preelection polls enjoy is based on the performance of a few national polling organizations in presidential elections, especially in the 1960, 1968, and 1976 elections, which were won by very narrow margins. In contrast, critics of polls point to elections in which polls have not been so accurate, especially the 1948 miscall of a Truman defeat and the 1980 final polls that indicated that the election (in which Reagan won a comfortable majority) was "too close to call."

In judging how accurate preelection polls are, we must first define what we mean by *accuracy*. It is not enough to call the winner. A poll that shows candidate A ahead by a margin of 60 percent to 40 percent when he or she wins by 51 percent to 49 percent is far less accurate than a poll that has candidate B ahead by 51 percent to 49 percent. The estimated percent of the vote for each candidate must be used to judge statistical accuracy; the key question is how much of a difference in percentage points exists between election returns and poll results. When this criterion is employed, we can use statistical theory to test whether a poll is accurate within the expected limits of sampling error—that is, whether the projected percent of the vote for a candidate is satisfactorily close to the percent he or she gets in the election. (Accuracy is not the same as *validity,* which has to do with whether the poll measures what it claims to be measuring. Thus, the questions asked in a poll may be valid in that they "really" measure voting intention, but, for a variety of reasons discussed later in this chapter, the poll may differ appreciably from election results and in that sense be inaccurate.)

Sampling Error

Sampling error does not refer to error in the everyday meaning of the word "mistake." Rather, it refers to the fact that when only part of a population is surveyed, the results cannot be expected to correspond exactly to what would have been obtained if everyone had been interviewed. Some divergence is inevitable. If a sample is selected so that everyone in the population has a known chance, or likelihood, of being selected—what statisticians call a *probability sample*—we can calculate how much divergence can be expected through chance alone. Those chance divergences are referred to as *sampling errors.* Divergences other than those due to chance—such as errors that result from biased or otherwise poorly designed questions, poorly trained interviewers, and mistakes in data processing—are *nonsampling errors.* A poll's *total* error is the *sum* of sampling and nonsampling errors.[3]

The distinction between sampling error and all other types of error must be kept in mind when evaluating the accuracy of preelection polls (in fact, all polls). Whereas allowances for sampling error can be calculated mathematically, that cannot be done for any type of nonsampling error. But the distinction between sampling and nonsampling error is usually confusing to nonstatisticians because *non*sampling error also includes *sample bias.* By sample bias statisticians mean the deviation of a sample from the population being surveyed that results when some people have a better chance of being selected than do others. For example, telephone surveys are susceptible to sample bias because people living in households with two or more telephone numbers have a greater chance of being selected than do members of one-telephone-number households, whereas members of nontelephone households have no chance at all of being selected.

One way of determining if a sample is biased is to compare its composition with known characteristics of the population being surveyed. By applying the appropriate statistical formulas, we can calculate whether the divergences that occur are ascribable to chance or whether they are so large that nonchance influences are probably at work. If they are that large, we can reasonably infer that the methods used to select the sample were in some way biased. If a nonprobability sampling procedure is used, the sample may through luck correspond fairly well to the population with regard to a few known characteristics and still be seriously biased on other, unknown characteristics. The latter characteristics normally include what the poll is intended to measure. To repeat, because allowances for sample bias cannot be mathematically calculated, polls based on *nonprobability samples* (samples that are selected using quotas and other nonprobability methods) are subject to sizable, unknown error due to sample bias. (Many polls are based on these samples.)

Similarly, we cannot calculate allowances for error resulting from such influences as biased question wordings or poor interviewing. For these reasons, when evaluating how accurate a poll is, we must keep in mind that accuracy depends upon the *combined* effects of sampling error plus all sources of nonsampling error. The California Poll makes this point very well in a sentence that it has used in its press releases: "Sampling error is not the only criterion, and we caution against citing only the sampling error figure alone as the measure of a survey's accuracy, since to do so tends to create an impression of a greater degree of precision than has in fact been achieved." In other words, when reading poll results, the allowance for sampling error is the *minimum* allowance for survey error, not the total allowance.

Inevitably, our discussion of sampling error must be technical, but no mathematics beyond simple arithmetic will be used. How much allowance to make for sampling error in any poll depends primarily upon (1) the size of the sample, (2) how certain the pollster wants to be about the results, and (3) how heterogeneous the population the pollster is sampling happens to be. (A fourth factor is the sample design, but this is a refinement with which we will not deal.) In polling, standard practice is to use a degree of certainty called the *95 percent confidence level.* At that level of certainty, we say that the chances are 95 in 100 that the stated allowance for sampling error will produce a conclusion that is correct.

The size of the sample

When calculating allowances for sampling error at any stated level of certainty, it is necessary to take the size of the sample into account. To give a concrete example, for polls based on simple random samples of about 1,200, at the 95 in 100 confidence level, allowances of plus or minus three percentage points would apply to percentages near 50 percent, whereas for samples of about 500 the allowance would be plus or minus six percentage points. Thus, if a poll based on a probability sample of 1,200 showed 52 percent in favor of a candidate, we can conclude that the chances are 95 in 100 that *if there was no nonsampling error,* the true figure is 52 percent plus or minus three percentage points—that is, between 49 percent and 55 percent. If the population is very homogeneous (for example, 90 percent favored one candidate), the allowance for sampling error would be smaller for each sample size.

If the results from this hypothetical poll differ from the election returns by more than three percentage points, that *additional* divergence is unlikely to be the result of sampling error but is almost certain to be due to nonchance sources of error. When actual divergences are larger than the allowance for sampling error, we have to look for nonsampling explanations of why that is the case. If the poll differs by less than three percentage points, that does *not* mean that the poll is more accurate than would be expected through chance. The allowance for sampling error defines the maximum range of expected divergence at some stated certainty level, or what statisticians call the *confidence band.* Most of the time actual divergences would be smaller than the maximum.

One especially confusing aspect of sampling error is that for all practical purposes, the size of the population being polled does not enter into the calculations (except when the sample comprises a large proportion of the population). Thus, how much to allow for sampling error normally depends on the size of the sample regardless of the size of the population being surveyed. The allowance for sampling error for a poll based on a sample of 1,000 is the same for Los Angeles, California, Sioux Falls, South Dakota, or the entire United States. Because this does not seem to make sense intuitively, many people mistakenly think that local polls can get away with sample sizes much smaller than those used by national polls. To the contrary, for any given level of accuracy, the same size sample is needed for a poll in a single congressional district as for the entire nation.

The magnitude of error

A study of the actual average performance of preelection polls reveals that the magnitude of error in preelection polls is far greater than is commonly realized. I examined the accuracy of 423 preelection polls— most of them on state and local elections and on primaries plus a few

TABLE 3.1
Accuracy of 423 Preelection Polls (in percentage point deviation of poll from election)

Accuracy	n	Range of Error	Average Error	Median Error
Most accurate one-third	141	0.10–3.04	1.55	1.65
Middle one-third	141	3.05–6.36	4.60	4.67
Least accurate one-third	141	6.40–29.50	10.86	9.42

Source: Irving Crespi, Pre-election Polling: Sources of Accuracy and Error (New York: Russell Sage Foundation, 1988), pp. 23–25.

national polls on presidential elections—conducted during the period 1979–1984.[4] The *average* difference between election returns and poll results in the percent of the vote received by the winning candidates in these 423 elections was 5.7 percentage points. Furthermore, as shown in Table 3.1, one-third of the polls deviated from the actual election returns by more than 6.4 percentage points.

Two observations about the high average error are pertinent. First, an average difference of 5.7 points is much larger than we would expect from the performance in presidential elections of the leading national polls. However accurate some polling organizations may be, most preelection polls have not been precision measuring instruments. Second, after entering the average sample sizes of those polls into our calculations, the actual average error of 5.7 points is about three times as large as what would be expected through chance alone.[5] In other words, the lack of precision in those 423 preelection polls cannot be explained only by sampling error. Much of their inaccuracy is due to nonsampling error. We have to look elsewhere than sampling error to explain the poor average performance of preelection polls.

Subgroups in the sample

Before doing that, however, there are other aspects of sampling error that merit our attention. First, allowances for sampling error for subgroups within a sample are considerably larger than for the total sample. For example, when poll results are reported by sex, age, party identification, ethnic origin, and educational achievement, the allowances for sampling error have to be computed using the sample sizes of each of those demographic segments. Using sex as an example, if the total sample is 1,200, it probably consists of approximately 600 women and men each. The sampling error allowance for men and women would in that case be plus or minus five percentage points as compared with plus or minus three percentage points for the entire sample. Even larger allowances would have to be made for smaller subgroups such as blacks or college graduates.

Polls with total samples of 500–750 are quite common, especially polls conducted on primaries as well as polls commissioned by local media or by politicians for their private use. In those cases, results for subgroups are often based on subsamples of about 100 cases each, and sometimes even less. With subsamples of that size, allowances for sampling error as large as plus or minus thirteen points would apply. Thus, for example, if a poll shows that 50 percent of 100 blacks prefer candidate A, the allowance for sampling error would give a range of between 37 percent and 63 percent as the true preference of blacks. Such a result is clearly of little value for drawing meaningful conclusions as to the voting proclivities of blacks. Nonetheless, many reported poll results for subgroups are subject to allowances for sampling error that are that large, with readers usually not informed of that fact. Most often, only the sampling error allowance for the total sample is reported by news media. (A few newspapers, such as the *New York Times,* do include in their reports a statement that larger allowances for sampling error should be applied to subgroups.) The potential for misinterpreting poll results is obviously quite large when only the allowance for the total sample is reported.

The percentage point margin

The picture is complicated even further by the now common practice of analyzing candidate standings in terms of the *spread,* or percentage point margin, between candidates. For instance, if a poll reports a five-point margin between two candidates when one is ahead by 52 percent to 47 percent (with 1 percent undecided), the allowances for sampling error we have been considering relate to the 52 percent and the 47 percent, but not to the five-point spread. If a nonstatistician is told that the poll results are subject to a sampling error of plus or minus four percentage points, he or she would undoubtedly infer that a five-point spread is statistically significant. In fact, a separate calculation would have to be made for the sampling error of the spread. As shown in Table 3.2, the allowance for sampling error of the 52 percent for candidate A is plus or minus 3.9 percentage points. But the sampling error allowance for the five-point spread between 52 percent and 47 percent (with a sample size of 1,000) is plus or minus 7.9 percentage points. In other words, with a sample size of 1,000, the five-point margin between 52 percent and 47 percent could have been expected through chance and is not statistically significant.

Only someone trained in statistical analysis will comfortably follow a technical discussion of sampling error such as has just been advanced.

TABLE 3.2
Allowance for Sampling Error for Selected Poll Results
(in percentage points) at the 95 in 100 Confidence Level, Assuming Sample Size of 1,000[a]

Hypothetical Poll Results (%)			Point Spread	Sampling Error Allowance for:	
Candidate A	Candidate B	Undecided	Between Candidates	Percent in favor of Candidate A	Point Spread
52	47	1	5[b]	±3.9	±7.9
48	42	10	6[b]	±3.9	±7.5
48	39	13	9	±3.9	±6.5
55	40	5	15	±3.9	±7.6

[a]A sample design effect of a 25 percent increase in sampling error is assumed.
[b]The odds are 95 in 100 that this point spread could have occurred through chance.

Others must rely on the pollster's skill and integrity to find out what conclusions can be validly drawn from poll results. All too often, however, because of an understandable desire not to confuse the audience, or because of pressure from news editors to ignore "academic niceties," or, regrettably, because some pollsters do not have the integrity or knowledge, these statistical fine points are often not considered when poll results are reported. Unwarranted and wrong interpretations of the political scene are the inevitable consequence. A sound understanding of what sampling error means, and does not mean, is essential to the proper use of poll data. Although it is unreasonable to expect most of the general public to have such an understanding, it is not unreasonable to ask that poll reports be written in a way that does not mislead readers about these statistical fine points.

Nonsampling Errors

When we turn to the nonchance factors that account for the large average error of preelection polls, a complete analysis would address a large number of influences, including some related to sample design and others related to nonsampling considerations. Sample design considerations focus primarily on controlling sample bias, which normally translates into the use of a probability sample design. In a probability sample, everyone in the total population has a known chance of being selected. To design such a sample requires using mathematically controlled procedures for selecting households, using a mathematically random selection procedure for determining who in a household should be interviewed instead of talking to whomever answers the telephone, and making follow-up calls to complete interviews with respondents who are not at home when interviewers call or when no one is at home. In telephone surveys, provision for reaching households with unlisted numbers must also be made.

Nonsampling considerations include such matters as question wording, the proportion of respondents who are undecided, whether any of the candidates are incumbents, and whether the election is a close one. Rather than attempting to deal with all those nonchance factors, I shall focus on two that are especially important in preelection polling—low turnout and the closeness of interviewing dates to the election.

Low turnout

One of the more significant nonchance influences on poll accuracy is the difficulty of dealing with turnout—specifically, of identifying which of all the persons interviewed who are eligible to vote do so. Probably the most important reason polls conducted immediately before the 1988 caucuses in Iowa and Michigan, in which tiny proportions of the total voting age populations participated, were not very accurate was the problem of identifying who would attend those caucuses.

A quantitative indicator of the impact of turnout rate on poll accuracy is the difference in accuracy of preelection polls conducted on high-turnout and low-turnout elections. In the study of poll accuracy mentioned earlier, of those polls that were conducted on elections in which more than one-half the electorate voted, 39 percent were of relatively high accuracy. In contrast, only 26 percent of polls conducted on elections in which less than one-third of the electorate voted were of high accuracy.[6] Most of those low-turnout elections were either primaries or off-year state and local elections.

The reason the ability to identify likely voters affects accuracy is that voters and nonvoters often (but not always) differ in their candidate preferences. Consequently, if nonvoters are included in polls of voter preferences, that could seriously distort estimates of a candidate's voting strength. The effect on accuracy of not screening out nonvoters is a major contributing factor to polling error in low-turnout elections such as primaries and off-year elections for state and local offices. But even in high-turnout presidential elections, screening out nonvoters contributes to accuracy.

Professional pollsters are in agreement that identifying who will vote is one of the most difficult tasks in preelection polling. Mervin Field of the California Poll has gone so far as to say that identifying likely voters is the weakest link in poll methodology. Pollsters use a variety of mostly crude methods to screen out nonvoters, although these methods are reasonably satisfactory for high-turnout elections. Only a few polling organizations have invested the time and money necessary to develop sophisticated methods for identifying likely voters, and those who have done so have achieved success only in high-turnout elections.[7]

Expecting polls on low-turnout primaries and off-year state and local elections to be as accurate as those conducted on high-turnout presidential elections is simply not warranted. Yet expectations regarding the accuracy of all polls are conditioned by the prominence of polls that, because they are on elections with high turnouts, have a relatively good chance of being accurate. Users of preelection poll results who do not understand the magnitude of error in polls that do not have satisfactory methods for dealing with turnout can be seriously misled when assessing the true voting strength of competing candidates.

Timing

Timing is an even more important factor influencing the accuracy of preelection polls. The Gallup Poll explained its seventeen-percentage-point error in the 1988 Republican New Hampshire primary as due to the fact that it stopped polling too soon. The CBS News/*New York Times* poll, which continued interviewing later in that primary than any other polling organization, was the only one that caught the last-minute surge that gave George Bush his victory over Robert Dole.[8] Similarly, many pollsters have said that a shift in voter preferences during the final campaign weekend in 1980 converted what had been a race "too close to call" into a solid Reagan victory.[9] One study on poll accuracy determined that only polls conducted very close to Election Day can be relied on, with any confidence, to provide a good estimate of the final election returns: Whereas 45 percent of the polls that were conducted within five days of the election were within three percentage points of election returns, only 24 percent of polls conducted thirteen days or more in advance achieved this degree of accuracy.[10]

The combined effects of timing and low turnout can be devastating in their effects on poll accuracy. Three polls conducted a week before the 1988 Michigan Democratic presidential caucuses either had Michael Dukakis and Jesse Jackson in a virtual tie or Dukakis slightly ahead.[11] As it turned out, Jackson outpolled Dukakis in those caucuses by a margin of two to one. Charles Hakes, whose company conducted one of those polls, observed later, "We can say how people think and what they say they intend to do 10 days before the event. We can't find out how people will change their minds 10 days hence."[12] Adam Clymer of the *New York Times,* commenting on those polls, said, "We should have reported the polls' findings about the preferences of those most likely to vote. But in any case, no poll, or other reporting, got at the fact that 2 of the 18 congressional districts, two all-black districts, would cast almost a quarter of the total vote."[13] In fact, the *Detroit Free Press* and the *Detroit News* both said their polls had indicated that Jackson was stronger than Dukakis when only likely voters were considered, but this significant finding apparently was overlooked in the reporting of the overall poll results.[14]

EARLY POLLS, VOLATILITY, AND DIAGNOSTICS

The reputation for accuracy that some pollsters have achieved is based entirely on polls that were conducted within the closing days of election campaigns. The obvious implications of this are ignored by those who believe that early polls can be used to predict election outcomes. That belief is based on the misapprehension that preelection polls predict how people will vote. *Polls do not predict.* Rather, they measure the preferences between candidates at the time interviews are conducted. Those who want to may then project those measurements into the future and then make predictions about elections. If a poll is conducted very close to Election Day, so that there is little time for preferences to change, such projections may be warranted. Otherwise, there is no reason to assume they will be accurate forecasts of election outcome.

Early Polls

The distinction between *prediction* and *projection* is fundamental to the valid interpretation of preelection polls. Politicians, political analysts, and financial contributors who act on the assumption that all preelection polls are as useful for predicting as are the handful of final polls on presidential elections make themselves vulnerable to serious errors.

Ever since 1948, when during the final weeks of the election campaign Harry Truman overcame Thomas Dewey's early lead, pollsters have repeatedly insisted that preelection polls are not predictions of how people will vote. Their previous experience, restricted to years in which Franklin D. Roosevelt was a candidate for reelection, had led many analysts of voting behavior to conclude that voting decisions were pretty much fixed once nominations had been made, with little subsequent change likely.[15] That may have been true so long as Roosevelt was a candidate—attitudes toward him were fixed, and most people knew whether they were for or against him once it was certain he would run for reelection.

It can still be true when a popular incumbent president runs for reelection. For example, in 1956 when Eisenhower ran for reelection and in 1984 when Reagan did, voting preferences as charted by polls conducted during the course of those campaigns were very stable. But other presidential elections—such as those in 1948, 1968, and 1980—were characterized by marked changes in voting preferences. Post-election analyses conducted by the CBS/*New York Times* Poll and the Gallup Poll indicated that during the last week of the 1980 campaign, enough voters changed their minds to transform what had been up to then a very close race into a decisive victory for Reagan.[16] In 1988, exit polls based on interviews with voters as they left their voting locations indicated that as many as one in six voters did not decide for whom to vote until the last week and that those late deciders voted for the loser Dukakis by a three to two ratio.[17]

Volatility

Volatility, continuing changes in voting preferences, has become a cliché in the reporting of preelection polls by the news media. Nonetheless, voting preferences are very stable in some elections and are subject to sizable swings in others. How volatile an election will be depends upon a number of factors: how well known the candidates are at the start of the campaign, the saliency and visibility of the election, how crystallized voter attitudes are, the influence of party identification on voting decisions, and the impact of events on voting decisions.

The candidates' name recognition

A candidate with high name recognition starts with a decided advantage, but that advantage can dissipate rapidly if he or she blunders or if the opposing candidate has the resources and uses them effectively. In 1987, early readings of voter preferences as to who should be the 1988 Democratic presidential candidate illustrate this point. At first, Gary Hart and Jesse Jackson, both of whom had achieved national prominence in the 1984 primaries, commanded double-digit support in preference polls among Democrats. All the other candidates, including the eventual nominee Michael Dukakis, languished far behind. After Hart's withdrawal, as the only remaining contender with a national reputation, Jackson continued to lead the other aspirants by a sizable margin. It was not until Dukakis gained the attention of the national news media by winning a series of state primaries that he moved strongly ahead in national preference polls.

A very different pattern existed in the 1988 Republican primary races. Vice-President George Bush and Senator Robert Dole (who had achieved national prominence in his role as Senate majority leader) each entered the 1988 presidential primaries with high name recognition. As was to be expected, initially preprimary polls showed them in close contention. But after Bush's "upset" victory in the New Hampshire Republican primary and his subsequent primary victories in the South, Bush steadily and inexorably moved into an unstoppable lead.

Similarly, the ability of a newcomer to politics with a well-known family name to retain an early lead depends on, among other things, the success with which he or she establishes a positive reputation, or image, of his or her own. Barry Goldwater, Jr., in his 1982 effort to receive the Republican nomination for U.S. senator from California, achieved impressive leads in early polls that progressively narrowed and eventually disappeared. In an earlier generation, the same happened with Franklin Roosevelt, Jr.'s candidacy for governor of New York. In contrast, Edward Kennedy, building upon a family name base, achieved a strong political identity of his own that made him unbeatable in his native state of Massachusetts.

The saliency and visibility of an election

Presidential elections receive extensive attention from the news media far in advance of an election, the preeminent significance of the office is recognized, and very large sums are expended on campaigning. Under those conditions, voting intentions often crystallize relatively early in the campaign. In such instances, an early poll might, in fact, give a good indication of the election outcome. (But even in elections for high office, if large segments of the electorate are not familiar with a candidate at the start of a campaign, initial preferences may be susceptible to considerable change.) This contrasts with elections for lesser offices and primaries, which typically do not receive much attention until the final days before election. In the latter type of election, many voters do not have voting intentions in any meaningful sense of the word until those final days before election, and even then their intentions may not be firm.

The degree of crystallization
of voter attitudes

Once it was confirmed in 1956 that Dwight Eisenhower was running again for president, and in 1984 that Ronald Reagan was, there was very little fluctuation in their poll standings. Most voters knew from the start whether they wanted those incumbents to win. The 1988 election campaign was very different, with neither Bush nor Dukakis evoking a clear public image until well into the fall. This accounts

TABLE 3.3
Variability in National Poll Measures of Voter Preference Between Bush and Dukakis

Surveys	Standard Error of the "Point Spread" Between Candidates
May (5 surveys)	3.0
June (6 surveys)	4.2
July (14 surveys)	6.1
August (13 surveys)	6.8
September (18 surveys)	3.9
October (pre-second debate; 10 surveys)	1.9
October (post-second debate; 14 surveys)	3.9

Source: Communication from Andrew Kohut, President, The Gallup Organization.

for the wide swings in their poll standings—from a seventeen-point spread in favor of Dukakis in some polls in the spring, to a seventeen-point spread in favor of Bush in one poll in mid-October, to Bush's final victory margin of eight points. The Gallup Poll's final preelection poll, based on interviewing conducted on the Friday, Saturday, and Sunday before Election Day, found that 20 percent of likely voters might still switch or were undecided in their preference.[18]

One objective indicator of crystallization in the 1988 presidential campaign is reported by Andrew Kohut of the Gallup Poll.[19] Taking the published results of the major media polls in successive time periods, he calculated the standard error of the point spread between Bush and Dukakis in each period as a measure of variability among polls (see Table 3.3). During the spring, a time when Dukakis had an apparently strong lead but prospective voters reported they did not know much about him, there was a moderately high degree of variability among those polls. During July and August, when the nominating conventions were being held and voters were changing their minds, variability among the polls virtually doubled. By mid-October, all the polls were in virtual agreement in their measurements of candidate standings, which suggested that preferences were crystallizing. But after the second televised debate between Bush and Dukakis, when Dukakis launched an aggressive counterattack that reduced Bush's lead, poll results became more variable. Thus, ignoring the chronology of crystallization and decrystallization in a campaign can lead to serious misinterpretation of what is happening.

Party identification

Party loyalty is a stabilizing influence on voting intentions. In the absence of any specific reason for doing otherwise, the voter's natural tendency is to vote for candidates of the party with which he or she identifies. Party loyalty, however, plays no role in primaries and non-partisan local elections, and polls conducted on such elections often register very large shifts in the last days of a campaign. The 1964 California primary in which Barry Goldwater surged ahead of Nelson Rockefeller over the final weekend, the 1984 New Hampshire primary in which Walter Mondale lost his sizable lead in early polls, and the 1988 New Hampshire primary in which Robert Dole lost a lead he had temporarily assumed after his victory in the Iowa caucus are typical of what can happen when party loyalty does not stabilize voting intentions. Since party loyalties weakened during the 1970s and 1980s, with more people calling themselves Independents than ever before, it may be that a decline of party loyalty was contributing to the volatility of all elections.

The impact of events

Anticipating the effect of events on voting decisions is virtually impossible. Whether it be a televised debate, the outbreak of conflict overseas, or the hint of scandal in a candidate's background, events can lead to marked shifts in voting intentions. Most pollsters have concluded that the last Carter-Reagan debate in 1980, combined with Carter's inability to resolve the Iranian hostage crisis during the final weekend of that campaign, contributed significantly to the size of Reagan's victory. But in 1984, Mondale's apparent superiority over Reagan in that year's first debate had a trivial, and transitory, effect on voting intentions. The effect of events on elections, let alone their occurrence, is imponderable, thereby making any effort to predict an election by projecting the results of early polls very questionable.

To interpret preelection polls realistically, we must recognize that the interaction of name recognition, saliency and visibility of an election, degree of crystallization, party identification, and events can be very complex. In some elections, that interaction may lead to the early crystallization of voting intentions. When that happens, early polls may provide surprisingly accurate indicators of election outcomes. But in many elections—especially, but not only, primaries and elections for low-visibility offices—voting intentions crystallize late. In late-crystal-lizing elections, early polls are highly unreliable for predicting how the electorate will vote.

Diagnostics

That is not to say that early polls have no value. To the contrary, they have considerable *diagnostic* value—if properly used. The goal of a valid analysis of early polls would be to identify a candidate's early sources of strength and weakness, not on the assumption that they will be immutable but in order to determine what kind of a campaign strategy is needed to win. For that purpose, the poll results could be analyzed to answer such questions as the following:

- How well known are the competing candidates in terms of name recognition, reputation, or image?
- If a potential candidate does well in an early poll, is that merely because he or she has a well-known name?
- If a candidate has a well-known name, what expectations do people have of someone with that name?
- If a candidate does poorly because he or she is not well known, how does the candidate fare among those who do know him or her, and why?
- How involved is the electorate in the office at stake, and what are the preferences of those to whom the election is important?
- How committed are adherents of the competing candidates to their current choices and, again, why?

These questions by no means exhaust what a diagnostic analysis would consider, but they do suggest the richness and political relevance of what might be attempted.

Many additional questions would be posed in a complete analysis of an early poll. But in any case, the purpose of the analysis would *not* be to predict who will win. Instead, the purpose would be to identify a candidate's strengths, decide how to capitalize on them, identify his or her weaknesses, and plan what to do to counteract them. A potential financial supporter might ultimately decide from a detailed analysis that the resources needed to get an aspiring candidate elected are greater than are available and might therefore decide not to support him or her. On the other hand, that supporter might also decide to do everything possible to obtain the needed resources because of a conviction that he or she is the best candidate. In either case, the decision would make use of a poll-based diagnosis of the situation, but it would not be based on a prediction naively projected from an early poll.

As an example of what might be learned from a diagnostic analysis of early poll results, consider the following data from a CBS News/ *New York Times* national poll.[20] This poll was conducted two months before the 1988 Iowa caucus—that is, at a time when even in the early primary states most voters were not paying much attention to the forthcoming elections. A series of questions asked for a favorable or unfavorable rating of the seven candidates who were then vying for the Democratic nomination—Jesse Jackson, Bruce Babbitt, Michael Dukakis, Dick Gephardt, Albert Gore, Paul Simon, and Gary Hart. To allow for the fact that many voters were not as yet familiar with some of the candidates, or else had not as yet formed an opinion about them, the question wording posed the possibility that the respondent was undecided or had not yet heard enough about a candidate to have an opinion.

A comparison of the ratings given to each candidate yields an incisive, and still concise, picture of their competitive positions—without falling into the trap of making premature predictions.

1. Only two candidates, Jackson and Hart, had achieved a high level of voter awareness. Ten percent had not heard enough about Jackson to have an opinion about him, as was the case for 7 percent with respect to Hart. This compares with a 53 percent nonrecognition for Dukakis, 51 percent for Gephardt, 55 percent for Gore, 49 percent for Simon, and 71 percent for Babbitt.

2. Jackson and Hart also stood out as the only two with a high proportion of unfavorable responses—34 percent for Jackson and 27 percent for Hart. To evaluate this result, it is best to consider the ratio of favorable to unfavorable responses as a way of taking into account differences in awareness. (For example, Dukakis and Babbitt were rated unfavorably by very similar proportions, although Dukakis was better known. Thus, relative to how many knew enough about each to rate them, Babbitt was more likely to be rated unfavorably than was Dukakis.) When the ratios are compared, Dukakis stands as the strongest, with a ratio of 24 percent favorable to 4 percent unfavorable. Simon ranks next with a ratio of 19 percent to 10 percent, followed by Gephardt with 11 percent to 8 percent, Gore with 10 percent to 10 percent, and Babbitt with 3 percent to 6 percent.

As these results show, each candidate faced a different challenge in his effort to receive the Democratic nomination. Although Jackson and Hart were each well known, each also had a serious problem in the large number who had negative attitudes. In contrast, Dukakis and Simon had the task of achieving voter awareness but could hope that if they were successful in that endeavor, a majority would view them favorably. Gore and Babbitt each had a still different problem—achieving voter awareness and also developing a favorable public persona.

The difference between using early polls as predictions or as diagnoses is clear in Roll's description of Howard Baker's use of an early poll when deciding to run for U.S. senator in 1966 against Frank Clement, the then incumbent governor of Tennessee.[21] As a well-known and popular incumbent, Clement ran twenty points ahead of Baker in a privately commissioned December 1965 poll, a lead large enough to have dissuaded most from attempting the race. But the report on that poll also suggested that Clement's tax policies made him vulnerable to an aggressive campaign. Baker entered the race and, as we know, went on to win despite what many would have considered insurmountable odds. More recently, Mario Cuomo overcame what appeared to be the even more formidable lead held by Edward Koch in early polls on the 1982 New York Democratic gubernatorial primary. According to pollster Gordon Black, Jewish voters, unfamiliar with Cuomo's issue orientation, initially were overwhelmingly for Koch, but as they learned more about Cuomo, many switched to him.[22] Instead of accepting those early polls as indicators of a lost cause, Cuomo's campaign staff successfully used them to help define what he had to do to win the primary.

Conducting a series of polls during the course of an election campaign in order to chart trends in voting preferences also has diagnostic value. The danger in this instance is the temptation to project trend lines into the future. Pollsters have learned that such projections can be very misleading because trend lines can reverse direction. In 1984, Mondale registered a small but real gain in polls taken immediately after his first debate with Reagan, but within a week those initial gains had dissipated. In 1980, no persistent trend in preference between Carter and Reagan existed before the last week of the presidential campaign, and it was not until that final week that a definitive move to Reagan occurred.

Significant ebbs and flows in voting preferences can also occur during the course of a campaign. One dramatic example was the movement toward and then away from George Wallace in the 1968 presidential election. At the midpoint of that campaign, polls conducted by the Gallup Poll averaged about 22 percent of the electorate voicing a preference for him. Much of that strength, however, shifted to Hubert Humphrey as the campaign reached its final stages, and Wallace ultimately got 13.6 percent of the national popular vote.[23]

The compulsion to use early polls to predict election outcomes is also manifest in attempts to identify correlations between polls conducted at a certain point in time before Election Day and the actual returns. During the spring of 1988, trial heats pitted the all-but-nominated George Bush, who had virtually retired from the campaign trail and did not resume vigorous campaigning until the August nominating convention, against Michael Dukakis, who was still actively campaigning against Jesse Jackson in order to achieve a majority of delegate votes before the Democratic convention in July. Those spring polls showed a decisive Dukakis margin of as large as seventeen percentage points. Some political analysts cited polls from earlier years in which whatever candidate was in the lead in the spring eventually won to conclude that Dukakis would win the November election.[24] But Dukakis's lead all but disappeared by August and Bush assumed the lead by the beginning of September. At that time, others declared Bush the winner, this time citing polls from earlier years that purportedly showed that whoever was ahead after both nominating conventions were over was the eventual winner.[25]

The early forecast of a Dukakis victory was, of course, disproved by Bush's election. Nevertheless, the forecast of a Bush victory based on August polling was equally flawed, as shown by Harry Truman's 1948 victory. On the other hand, Humphrey's fifteen-point resurgence in October 1968 was almost enough to win him the election and was greater than the points Dukakis needed to wipe out Bush's lead in September 1988. In the event, Bush's lead widened dramatically in October and then narrowed somewhat during the final weeks of the campaign. There is no magic formula for predicting elections from trends in past campaigns.

Changes in voting intentions often occur in irregular patterns, so that simple projections cannot be relied on. The proclivity of some politicians and financial backers to decide which candidates to support on the basis of early polls reveals their ignorance of the inherent limitations of polls for predicting, as distinct from diagnosing, voting behavior. Fostering a sound understanding of those limitations would contribute far more to the responsible use of polls than exhorting politicians and financial backers to support good, rather than merely popular, candidates. Most importantly, a sound understanding of the limitations of early polls requires an appreciation that voting intentions are not something cast in concrete. Rather, they are a kaleidoscope of the ever-changing desires, beliefs, values, and feelings of a heterogeneous public.

POLLING ON ISSUES
VERSUS BEHAVIORAL INTENTIONS

Although polls on voting intentions have set the tone for public opinion polling in general, the distinction between measuring voting intentions and measuring opinion on issues is one that needs to be made unequivocably. Assuming that experience in measuring voting intentions can be applied directly to investigating opinions confuses two different aspects of public opinion. Psychologically and behaviorally there is much that differentiates intentions to vote for a candidate from opinions regarding issues, including issues that figure prominently in an election.

Opinions on issues do not in themselves have a concrete behavioral component, although they may ultimately significantly influence behavior. An individual can have opinions, even strong opinions, regarding tax reform, disarmament, trade with Japan, sanctions against South Africa, abortion, gun control, the death penalty, pornography, or the 55-mph speed limit without feeling he or she has to act on them. Opinions as such are judgments on an issue, not statements about intentions to act. On occasion, individuals are called upon, or feel compelled, to act upon their opinions by voting, contributing to a cause, writing to their representatives, or participating in a public demonstration. Those actions are not opinions in themselves but the outcomes of opinions. By the same token, intentions to act, such as voting intentions, are not opinions but outcomes.

The distinction between opinions and intentions is made very clear when we compare answers to questions that ask whether a respondent approves of the way an incumbent president is handling his job and those that ask whether a respondent would vote for him or his opponent if, as the latter questions are typically phrased, the election were held today. Polling experience is that more people say they approve of a president's performance in office than say they would vote for him.[26] A voter may judge that an incumbent is doing a satisfactory job as president but, for any number of reasons, prefer someone else as president and therefore vote against the incumbent. Conversely, a voter may dislike an incumbent but, because of party loyalty, vote for his reelection.

The absence of a specific behavioral component in opinions makes all the difference when evaluating the accuracy and validity of polls on issues. Regarding accuracy, the allowance that should be made for sampling error is the same whether opinions or voting intentions are being measured. In both cases, the likely range of sampling error can be calculated. When measuring opinions, however, there is no behavioral act with which responses can be compared and validated. This contrasts sharply with polls on voting intentions, which can be compared with election returns. If two polls are conducted on the day before an election and the results of one are two percentage points different from the election returns while the other differs by eight percentage points, it would be reasonable to conclude that the former is more accurate. But if two polls taken on the same day differ in the proportion that approve an incumbent president's performance in office, there is no meaningful external criterion for deciding which is the more accurate.

Instead, the design—especially with respect to question wording—and implementation of the two polls have to be examined to see if any judgment of their comparative accuracy can be made.

From time to time polls that ask for an evaluation of a president's performance in office have differed to a degree that is statistically significant, even when interviewing for the two polls was carried on concurrently. Two reasons this happens relate to question wording. One relates to differences in the rating scale respondents are asked to use for evaluating the incumbent's performance and the other to the substantive content of the question.

First, some polls ask simple, *dichotomous questions*—do you approve or disapprove?—whereas others ask respondents to use some type of *rating scale*. As Gary Orren and Barry Sussman have shown, the proportion that rates a president favorably will differ depending on whether a dichotomous question or a rating scale is used.[27] They compared the results of three question wordings on presidential approval: (1) the dichotomous question asked by Gallup—"Do you approve or disapprove of the way Jimmy Carter is handling his job as president?" with a follow-up "Is that approve/disapprove strongly or approve/disapprove somewhat?" (2) the four-point rating scale used by Harris—"How would you rate the job Jimmy Carter is doing as president? Would you say he is doing an excellent, pretty good, only fair, or a poor job?" and (3) the five-point rating scale used by the *Washington Post*—"Suppose you were to grade President Carter A, B, C, D, or F for the way he is handling his job as president. What grade would you give him?" The Gallup question produced an approval rating for Carter of 62 percent. In comparison, the Harris question yielded 48 percent excellent or pretty good and 49 percent only fair or poor. The *Post* question results were 41 percent A or B, 35 percent C, and 17 percent D or F. As this experiment shows, the number of positions on a rating scale significantly affects how favorably a president is rated.

Because the Harris and *Post* questions have more than three points on a rating scale, the pollster must decide what *cutting point* to use when differentiating favorable and unfavorable ratings: that is, the point on the rating scale to use when distinguishing between favorable and unfavorable ratings. For example, with respect to the five-point scale used by the *Washington Post,* some argue that only a rating of A should be treated as favorable and that A and B responses should not be combined into a total "favorable" response. Marketing research experience is relevant to this argument. A common practice in marketing research studies of buying intentions is to use *top-box* scores—the percentage of respondents rating a product or brand in the most favorable category on the rating scale—not to combine moderately favorable responses with top-box responses.[28] Moderately favorable responses are "easy" to give, implying no behavioral commitment. Top-box responses, in contrast, tend to involve sufficient commitment, so that there usually is a sharp contrast in the buying behavior of those who give strongly favorable and moderately favorable ratings. In my experience in marketing research, the buying behavior of those who give moderately favorable responses is usually closer to those who give neutral ratings than to those who give strongly favorable ratings. Accordingly, polls on presidential approval might be far more revealing of public attitudes if instead of a single favorable percentage, they were to report two percentages—"strong approval" and "moderate approval."

The same principle holds for all polls that use rating scales. Lee Sigelman and Stanley Presser have shown how much of a difference the choice of cutting points can make by comparing what happens when only top-box cutting points are used to estimate the proportion of Americans who can be classified as supporters of the "New Christian Right."[29] They reanalyzed 1977 poll results from which John Simpson had estimated that 27 percent of the U.S. public supported the New Christian Right,[30] using only "strongly agree" response categories. When they did this, they classified only 9 percent as supporters. They concluded that any single estimate of how many people can be classified as supporters "is a function, among other things, of the manner in which a researcher treats the response categories on the items in question. Since there is no single 'correct' way to define cutting points, it follows that there is no single 'correct' point estimate."[31] More generally, no single percentage can be correctly said to represent public opinion. (We shall return to this principle.)

Second, questions differ in their substantive content. Gallup asks for a rating of job performance: "Do you approve or disapprove of the way (incumbent) has been handling his job as president?" In contrast, Roper asks whether the respondent supports the president: "How do you feel about President (incumbent)? At the present time, would you describe yourself as a strong (incumbent) supporter, a moderate (incumbent) supporter, a moderate critic of (incumbent), or a strong critic of (incumbent)?" These two questions tap different aspects of attitudes; a respondent can approve a president's recent actions and therefore respond favorably to Gallup's question but still oppose the president's overall policies and therefore respond unfavorably to Roper's question. It is not surprising that Roper's ratings of presidential standing are typically lower than those reported by Gallup.[32]

QUESTION ORDER

The order in which questions are asked can also affect poll results regarding candidate standings and opinions. A case in point is a conflict between two polls that measured voting intentions early in a campaign.[33] In early October 1982, the *New York Times* and the *Hartford Courant* concurrently conducted polls on that year's gubernatorial and senatorial elections in Connecticut. The two polls were in almost perfect agreement on the gubernatorial standings but differed on the senatorial race. As polling was conducted about four weeks before the election and a comparison of poll results with election results would therefore be incorrect for determining accuracy, the methodologies of the two polls were reviewed instead.[34] This review revealed that, among other things, the *Times* asked for preference on the gubernatorial race first whereas the *Courant* asked the senatorial question first.

Suspecting that the reversal in question order might be responsible for the conflict, the *Times* conducted a second poll in which half the sample was asked the gubernatorial question first and half the senatorial question first.[35] In that second poll, question order affected the senatorial but not the gubernatorial standings. We concluded that this was the probable explanation for the original conflict, but we had no way of determining from that experiment by itself which question order gave the more accurate measure of voting intentions when the original polls were conducted. Without an external criterion, deciding which is the more accurate could be based only by a personal judgment of which question wording was "better."

The order in which candidate names appear within a question may also significantly influence poll results. In a September 1988 poll on preferences between George Bush and Michael Dukakis, Roper found that when Dukakis's name was presented first, he had a twelve point lead over Bush but that when Bush's name was first, Dukakis's lead was cut to a mere four points.[36] Philip Meyer of the University of North Carolina discovered a similar effect of order of presentation in a poll he had conducted on the Bush-Dukakis race.[37] Again, without some external criterion (perhaps conformity with the order in which candidate names appear on the ballot on Election Day), no objective basis exists for saying which order provides the more accurate measurement of opinion. Sensitivity to the fact that such apparently minor considerations can significantly alter poll results is essential to the valid interpretation of poll results.

Polls on the 1988 presidential election reveal still another way in which the manner in which candidates are presented in questions may affect results. The *Los Angeles Times* conducted an experiment in a poll designed to measure whether the nomination of Dan Quayle to be Bush's running mate was likely to have an effect on the preferences of voters. Half the sample was asked for their preference between Bush and Dukakis, with no mention of the vice-presidential candidates. The other half was asked the same question, but with the names of the full ticket for each party—Bush/Quayle and Dukakis/Bentsen—included in the question. Bush led Dukakis by nine points when only their names were used but by only three points when the full tickets were named.[38] This difference was particularly surprising because experience in past elections had indicated that vice-presidential candidates had no noticeable effect on voting preferences. In 1988, however, the controversy concerning Quayle's qualifications apparently did have some effect. Only if questions are worded to cover all salient aspects of an issue—in this case, worded to cover the controversy about Quayle's qualifications—will they provide a valid measurement of opinion. (We will return to this point a bit later.)

GENERAL VERSUS SPECIFIC OPINIONS

A very important aspect of question wording is whether an issue is posed in general or specific terms. Consider, for example, the results of a poll on the political beliefs of the U.S. public conducted in the 1960s by Hadley Cantril and Lloyd Free.[39] They took two very different approaches to measuring how conservative or liberal Americans were at that time. In the first, they asked whether the respondent agreed or disagreed with a number of ideologically worded statements, such as "We should rely more on individual initiative and ability and not so much on government welfare programs." In the second approach, they measured approval of specific government programs, such as "a compulsory medical insurance program covering hospital and nursing care for the elderly." Replies to each series of questions were tallied for each individual interviewed in the poll. Based on those tallies, each individual was classified as completely or predominantly liberal, middle of the road, or completely or predominantly conservative. This classification was done separately for the ideological series of questions and for the issue series. The results could not be more different.

In regard to the ideological series, 16 percent were completely or predominantly liberal, and 50 percent were completely or predominantly conservative. But in regard to the series on specific programs, 65 percent were completely or predominantly liberal, and only 14 percent were completely or predominantly conservative. Interestingly enough, of the ideological conservatives, 46 percent were classified as liberals

TABLE 3.4
Liberalism-Conservatism on Ideological and Programmatic Levels (in percentages)

	Ideological		Specific Programs	
Completely liberal	4	16	44	65
Predominantly liberal	12		21	
Middle-of-the-road		34		21
Predominantly conservative	20	50	7	14
Completely conservative	30		7	

Source: Charles W. Roll, Jr., and Albert H. Cantril, *Polls: Their Use and Misuse in Politics* (New York: Basic Books, 1972), p. 123. © 1972 by Basic Books, Inc. Reprinted by permission of Basic Books, Inc., Publishers.

on the series of questions on specific government programs (see Table 3.4).

Two Gallup Polls, conducted in April and May 1986, found a comparable contrast regarding opinions on a variety of issue areas. When asked to classify themselves in terms of their political views, 20 percent rated themselves as liberals. This compares with 11 percent who rated themselves as liberal regarding their values about such matters as sex, morality, family life, and religion.[40] Similarly, in a confidential poll of middle- and upper-income people that I worked on for a private sector client, two questions were asked regarding liberalism-conservatism. One asked people to classify themselves as liberal, moderate, or conservative on economic issues, and the other asked for a similar rating on social issues. Twenty-seven percent classified themselves as liberals on economic issues, compared with 41 percent who did so on social issues.

As these comparisons show, whether a person is a liberal or conservative depends very much on the context of the question—liberal or conservative about what and as a general principle or on a specific issue. There is no simple answer as to what the political coloration of the public is at any point in time or how that coloration may be changing.

SENSITIVITY TO VARIATIONS IN QUESTION WORDING

Polling experience during the Watergate controversy provides an excellent illustration of how variations in question wording can lead to very large differences in poll results. In a single month, November 1973, four polling organizations asked six differently worded questions in seven different polls about whether Richard Nixon should be impeached or should resign.[41] The proportion in favor ranged from a low

TABLE 3.5
Effect of Question Wording on Approval of Impeaching Richard Nixon in Polls Conducted in November 1973

Question Wording	Proportion in Favor of Impeachment (%)
Would you like to see Nixon continue in office, decide to resign, or be impeached? (Yankelovich)	10
Do you think President Nixon should be impeached and compelled to leave office or not? (Gallup)	35/37[a]
[Following a list of possible criticisms or charges against Nixon, which respondents rated for seriousness for his possible responsibility] Because of the various charges that have recently been made against President Nixon, do you think impeachment proceedings should be brought against him or not? (Roper)	32
In view of what happened in the Watergate affair, do you think President Nixon should resign or not? (Harris)	43
Because of the various charges that have recently been made against President Nixon, do you think impeachment proceedings should be brought against him or not? (Roper)	47
If the Senate Watergate Committee decides that President Nixon was involved in the coverup, do you think Congress should impeach him, or not? (Harris)	53

[a]Gallup conducted two polls in which this question was asked.

Source: Gladys Engel Lang and Kurt Lang, The Battle for Public Opinion (New York: Columbia University Press, 1983), p. 116. Copyright © 1983 Columbia University Press. Used by permission.

of 10 percent to a high of 53 percent (see Table 3.5). These differences are almost completely ascribable to variations in question wording. The low of 10 percent was the proportion who favored impeachment in response to the question asked by Yankelovitch, "Would you like to see Nixon continue in office, decide to resign, or be impeached?" The high of 53 percent was the proportion who answered in favor of impeachment in a Harris poll that asked, "If the Senate Watergate Committee decides that President Nixon was involved in the cover-up, do you think Congress should impeach him or not?"

Of particular note is the fact that when Harris and Roper each varied their question wordings, they got different results. Thus, when Harris asked, "In view of what happened in the Watergate affair, do you think President Nixon should resign or not?" 43 percent favored resignation. This compares with 53 percent that favored impeachment in answer to the other Harris question. On the other hand, Gallup conducted two polls in November, one early in the month and one late, in which the same question was asked: "Do you think President Nixon should be impeached and compelled to leave office or not?" The proportion who answered yes was 35 percent in early November and 37 percent in late November, a difference that is statistically insignificant.

Jim Davis, a sociologist from the National Opinion Research Center (NORC), has observed that the sensitivity of poll results to the specific wording of questions is reassuring to anyone who wants to use polls to investigate public opinion. This sensitivity shows that people pay attention to the questions they are asked on polls. If variations in question wording did not make a difference, we would have to conclude that respondents to polls do not listen very carefully to what they are asked and therefore that their answers do not mean very much. What does happen is that sometimes variations in question wordings make a difference, and sometimes they do not.

Elisabeth Noelle-Neumann has investigated the conditions under which wording makes little difference.[42] She concluded that when opinions on an issue have crystallized, modifications in question wording have little effect on how questions are answered. But when opinions are not firm, variations in question wording that emphasize one or another aspect of an issue will have a marked effect on how questions are answered.

SINGLE VERSUS MULTIPLE QUESTIONS

The principle, applied during the 1940s by Louis Guttman, that any one question asked in a survey is a sample of all possible questions that could be asked must also be considered.[43] As Guttman pointed out, there are many different ways of posing an issue, each highlighting a different facet. Thus, no one question can possibly encompass the fullness of opinion on a given issue. Guttman concluded that only by asking a series of questions on an issue and then analyzing the pattern of responses to that series could a valid understanding of public opinion be developed. He developed rigorous statistical techniques for that purpose.

Even without Guttman's statistical techniques, asking more than one question on an issue and then cross-analyzing the results can clarify the meaning of poll results. Consider the results of two polls conducted in 1977 related to the issue of how much effort, if any, should be made to provide economic assistance to blacks. In the spring of that year, the National Opinion Research Center asked, "Are we spending too much, too little, or about the right amount on . . . improving the conditions of blacks?" Twenty-five percent said too little, 42 percent said about the right amount, 25 percent said too much, and 8 percent said they did not know. Just a few months later, in June of 1977, Roper asked, "Do you think _____ is something the government should be making a major effort on now, or something the government should be making some effort on now, or something not needing any particular government effort now . . . in trying to solve the problems caused by ghettos, race, and poverty?" In answer to that question, 66 percent said they thought a major effort should be made, 27 percent said some effort, 5 percent said no effort, and 3 percent had no opinion.[44]

The replies to the NORC question could be interpreted to mean that most Americans were then opposed to large government expenditures for economic assistance to blacks, whereas the Roper poll could be interpreted to mean that most were in favor of such expenditures. This apparent conflict could be resolved by other interpretations. For example, that a majority might have felt that a major effort was needed but that it was being made so that no increase was needed. Another possibility might be that many respondents understood the phrase "problems caused by ghettos, race and poverty" in the Roper question to include crime, a major concern of many Americans at that time. In that case, the majority support for a major effort might have related more to programs designed to reduce crime than to financial assistance. If both questions had been asked on the same poll, it would have been possible to cross-analyze responses so as to determine, for example, how many people who felt a major effort was needed also felt that about the right amount of money was being spent. Without such cross-analyses, the full meaning of those apparently conflicting poll results cannot be determined, and we can only speculate.

Using Biased Questions

Interestingly, a lot can be learned by asking a question that most would agree is biased, but only if it is part of a series of questions that vary in their strength and direction of bias. (This questioning strategy is essential to one analytic technique developed by Guttman.[45]) By itself that biased question would produce a misleading picture of public opinion, but as part of a series of questions it could have considerable analytic value. For example, if a question worded to elicit a positive response is answered positively by 55 percent of a sample, it would be wrong to conclude that a majority endorsed that positive view. But if a question equally biased in the negative direction elicited a positive response of 20 percent, the contrast between 55 percent and 20 percent would tell us something about the strength of commitment to the positive viewpoint. We could legitimately infer that the 20 percent who responded positively to the negatively biased question were strongly committed to their position. On the other hand, the difference between 20 percent and 55 percent would suggest that another 35 percent constituted a "swing" vote whose opinions were subject to change depending on the circumstances.

Using Single, "Balanced" Questions

In contrast to Guttman's approach, the typical goal in polling has been to develop single questions whose wording is balanced, giving equal weight to both sides of an issue, so as not to bias responses in one direction or another. Answers to such presumably unbiased questions are then interpreted as valid, summary measures of how opinion splits on an issue. The implicit assumption of this practice is that issues have a single core aspect and that public opinion divides in respect to that core aspect. But this is seldom the case.

On an issue such as abortion, for example, we might ask the simple question, "Do you favor or oppose a constitutional amendment forbidding abortion?" That question in itself appears to be unbiased: It offers both a positive and negative response, avoiding the possibly leading effect of asking only whether a person favors such an amendment. The terseness of the question also contributes to its balance by reducing the possibility that bias will result from highlighting one side's position rather than the other's or from misstating the arguments of either side.

Nonetheless, proponents of legal abortion could argue that posing the issue in terms of the adoption of a constitutional prohibition against abortion has a latent bias in that it gives salience to action favored by antiabortionists. A better question, they might argue, would be, "Do you favor a constitutional amendment forbidding abortion, or do you think the decision on whether to have an abortion should be left to the woman and her physician?" Antiabortionists, however, might respond by claiming that this alternative gives undue weight to the arguments of those who favor the right to have an abortion and that, in fact, the issue is whether the amendment should be adopted. No one question can measure how the public splits on whether a constitutional ban should be adopted. Furthermore, depending upon how crystallized the opinions of individual respondents might be, different wordings could produce apparently conflicting results.

We also have to consider the fact that opinions on legalized abortion are for many dependent on the surrounding circumstances.[46] (See Chapter 4 for details of poll results.) The proportion who would accept legalized abortion during the first trimester is greater than for the last trimester. The acceptability of abortion also varies depending upon whether it is for a woman who was raped, an unmarried teenager, a woman whose life is at risk, or an older married woman who does not want any more children. There are, of course, those who oppose legalized abortion under all circumstances, as there are those who oppose any legal restrictions on the right to have an abortion. Posing the issue in terms of whether a person believes life begins at conception will get different responses than when it is posed in terms of the individual woman's right to the privacy of her body. Only if all those questions are asked, and then analyzed in relation to each other, will a poll give us a valid understanding of public opinion regarding abortion.

Another example of what can be learned when polls investigate opinion in depth is a poll conducted by the *Los Angeles Times* in March 1989.[47] This poll revealed the complexity of attitudes regarding abortion and the conflicts that most Americans experience regarding its acceptability. On one hand, only 28 percent favored "an amendment to the United States Constitution that would prohibit abortions," while 62 percent opposed such an amendment (10 percent had no opinion). On the other hand, in that same poll, only 46 percent were in "favor of the Supreme Court decision which permits a woman to get an abortion from a doctor at any time within the first three months of her pregnancy," while 35 percent were opposed (19 percent had no opinion). Other results from that poll document further the extent to which majority opinion accepted legal abortion under certain circumstances, but with strong moral reservations:

- 88 percent said that if a "woman's health is seriously endangered by a pregnancy . . . it should be possible for a woman to obtain a legal abortion," 6 percent said it should not, and 6 percent did not express an opinion.
- 74 percent agreed with the statement "I personally feel that abortion is morally wrong, but I also feel that whether or not to have an abortion is a decision that has to be made by every woman for herself," 21 percent disagreed, and 5 percent had no opinion.
- 73 percent said that "if it came down to a question of saving the life of the mother or of the baby" they would save the mother's life, 8 percent said they would save the baby's life, and 19 percent did not express an opinion.
- 51 percent agreed with the statement "I am in favor of abortion because every woman has the right to control her own body," 44 percent disagreed, and 5 percent had no opinion.
- 38 percent favored "using public funds for abortions when the mother cannot afford it," 52 percent were opposed, and 10 percent had no opinion.

- 57 percent agreed with the statement "Abortion is murder," 35 percent disagreed, and 8 percent had no opinion.
- 61 percent said they believe abortion is morally wrong, 22 percent said that it is morally right, and 17 percent had no opinion.

Unfortunately, polls seldom ask a full series of questions on any one issue.[48]

Using Yes-No Questions

Pollsters who seek one question that will provide an unbiased, objective measure of opinion on abortion, or on any issue, implicitly if not explicitly assume that elections are the appropriate model for measuring public opinion. This conforms to Gallup's early view (see Chapter 1) that polls should serve as quasireferenda that instruct legislators on how to vote. In an election, each voter has to select one candidate to vote for or else abstain from voting. Therefore, when measuring candidate strength in polls, asking a straightforward voting preference question is unquestionably valid. A yes-no question would also be valid if all we want to know is how the public is likely to vote in a referendum on an issue. (Although, for a number of reasons, polls on referenda have a far worse accuracy record than do polls on candidates. Furthermore, when polling on a referendum, the question wording must correspond as closely as possible to the issue as defined on the ballot if the poll is to have any chance of providing an accurate indicator of voting behavior. Arguments about possible bias in question wording are irrelevant except as they relate to how well the question asked in the poll parallels the question on the ballot.)

However, the opinions that *underlie* voting behavior cannot be ascertained by a single question. A battery of questions must be asked to find out why people vote as they do. Similarly, reporting the responses to any one opinion question as if it summarizes the complexity of public thinking (or, for that matter, an individual's thinking) on an issue presents a biased picture, no matter how unbiased that question is in and of itself. If polls are to perform the function that Gallup set for them a half-century ago—that is, to act as a conduit through which public opinion can make itself known directly and objectively—they must do more than ask single yes-no questions on an issue.

In the same vein, it is not sufficient to know that an overwhelming majority of Americans say they favor a nuclear disarmament treaty with the Soviet Union. Concern about related issues such as the possibility that the Soviet Union would cheat and the fear that the United States may be militarily weaker than the Soviet Union must also be taken into account. By the same token, it is not sufficient to know that a majority favors a policy of providing welfare assistance to the poor. Beliefs regarding the incidence of welfare cheating, resentment about how tax burdens and benefits are distributed, and willingness to assume additional tax obligations must also be considered. Reagan's ability to attract votes from an electorate whose majority expressed sympathy for the needs of the poor cannot be explained unless considerations such as these are taken into account. In these, as in so many instances, what the public really wants and will support cannot be discovered by simply asking questions modeled on what is asked in polls on voting intention.

AWARENESS AND INVOLVEMENT

Another consideration is whether the opinions of the entire public are sampled or only of those who indicate some awareness or involvement in an issue. In an NBC News Poll conducted in May 1979, 79 percent reported they had not heard or read enough about the SALT II treaty to have an opinion on it. Of the rest, 13 percent favored the treaty and 6 percent opposed it (with 2 percent not giving any response at all). Another poll, also conducted by NBC News a month earlier in April 1979, asked *everyone* in the sample if he or she favored or opposed SALT II without first determining awareness of the controversy surrounding the treaty. In that poll, supporters outnumbered opponents 71 percent to 18 percent, a much larger ratio in favor than in the May poll.[49]

NBC News repeated both questions on two later polls, each about six months after the original polls.[50] The question that measured opinion only among those who were aware of the SALT II treaty registered a drop in the unaware group from 79 percent to 44 percent, along with a doubling in the proportion in favor from 13 percent to 25 percent and a quadrupling of those opposed from 6 percent to 26 percent. If we rely on that question, we would conclude that the opinions of the informed public had shifted and were now evenly split—25 percent versus 26 percent—on whether the treaty should be ratified. In contrast, if we relied on the question asked of the total sample, which also registered increased opposition—from a ratio of 71 percent to 18 percent in favor of ratification in the spring to 62 percent to 30 percent in the fall, we would conclude that in the fall the public still favored ratification by a two to one ratio. A more careful comparison of the two sets of polls, however, shows that the conflict between these two sets of poll results is more apparent than real.

To reconcile these seemingly contradictory results, we should note that although in the spring most of the public was not really involved in the debate about SALT II, if forced to express an opinion the majority favored ratification by a ratio of three to one. However, as awareness of the issue increased during the summer and into the fall, opposition also increased to 26 percent using the former question and to a similar 30 percent using the latter. That is to say, as the initially uninformed segment of the public became involved in the SALT II debate, many who at first initially expressed a positive opinion moved into the opposition camp. Apparently, opponents to ratification were more effective than proponents in reaching and persuading the heretofore uninvolved segment of the public.

It is not often that trends in public opinion are measured by two different questions, one of which filters out the unaware or uninvolved while the other does not. More commonly, questions make no attempt to screen out the unaware and uninvolved, so that poll results are presumably applicable to the total public. However, that presumption more often than not leads to a wrong assessment of public opinion. In the spring of 1979, a correct assessment of public opinion regarding SALT II would have stressed that a large segment of the public was favorably predisposed toward some kind of nuclear agreement between the United States and the Soviet Union but that many of those people were uninformed about SALT II. The approval of SALT II voiced by this segment of the public is more of a generalized sentiment in favor of defusing the arms race than an opinion on the treaty and its provisions. There can be value in learning about generalized sentiments and predispositions, but they should not be treated as equivalent to the views of those who have been following an issue and have developed a specific opinion on it.

A December 1987 Gallup Poll asked, "Next week President Reagan and Soviet leader Gorbachev are scheduled to sign a treaty that would eliminate all short- and intermediate-range nuclear missiles from Europe and the Soviet Union. Do you approve or disapprove of this treaty?"[51] Seventy-four percent said they approved. The news release reporting this endorsement contrasted it with a June 1979 Gallup Poll in which only 39 percent said they would like to see the Senate ratify the SALT II treaty. But the two polls were not directly comparable because, apart from differences in question wording, the 1979 measurement was based on about two-thirds of the total sample that was informed about the controversy surrounding ratification of the SALT II treaty.[52] Furthermore, it is not clear whether support for the Intermediate-range Nuclear Forces Treaty means that the public favored the specific provisions of the treaty rather than, for example, public faith in Ronald

Reagan as president compared with a lack of confidence in Jimmy Carter in 1979. Again the question arises as to whether a poll is measuring general sentiment or committed opinion.

GENERALIZED SENTIMENT
VERSUS COMMITTED OPINION

Pollsters have experimented with a number of ways for differentiating between generalized sentiments and committed opinions. Questions that ask about the perceived effectiveness of suggested policies and not merely whether one favors or opposes it—for example, whether the SALT Treaty is an effective way to reduce international tension and control the arms race—can be very useful for this purpose. Furthermore, those who believe a proposed course of action will be effective are far more likely to take a committed stand in its favor than those who favor it because they endorse its purposes but doubt its effectiveness. Unfortunately, this type of question is seldom asked in polls.

Another approach is to ask whether an opinion is strongly held. Presumably, those who claim that they strongly hold to a position are expressing a conviction that goes beyond mere sentiment. But such avowals of commitment leave room for doubt regarding readiness to stick to a position in the face of conflicting interests. One type of question that is occasionally used to relate voiced opinions to behavior in a convincing and politically relevant way asks whether a person is willing to pay increased taxes in order to implement his or her opinion. In a poll on the quality of New Jersey public schools conducted by The Eagleton Institute of Politics at Rutgers University, 52 percent said they would vote in favor of raising taxes if their "local public schools said they needed more money," and 34 percent said that they would vote against raising taxes.[53] This result is far more convincing evidence of public readiness to increase school budgets than if the question had asked only if a request for more money from local public schools should be granted.

Although asking about willingness to pay taxes is a valid way of measuring strength of opinion, this technique by itself does not determine whether a question gets at specific opinions or generalized sentiments. Consider the question "Would you be willing to pay more taxes to help raise the standards of education in the United States?" The majority willing to pay higher taxes rose from 58 percent in 1983 to 64 percent in 1988.[54] But these results offer no guidance regarding public opinion on how those additional tax monies should be spent— to raise teacher's salaries, to build new physical plants, to reduce the size of classes, to enrich science and foreign language curriculums, to expand preschool programs such as Head Start, to expand sports programs, to impose more stringent discipline in schools, or what? As it stands, this poll does no more than tell us that a sizable, increasing majority of Americans are sufficiently concerned about educational standards to say they are willing to pay increased taxes. It tells us nothing about what the public thinks are the root causes of the deficiencies in educational standards and how they should be dealt with.

TECHNICAL TERMINOLOGY

A particularly difficult problem in developing question wordings is how to deal with the special and technical terminology that often characterizes public debate. Terms such as strategic nuclear weapons, Soviet dissidents, détente, impeachment, budget deficit, and revenue sharing are familiar terms to those involved in those issues, but they are not readily understood by large segments of the public. Screening out those who report they have not been following an issue is one way of handling the problem of comprehension, but screening does not necessarily assure that those left in the sample will understand the special terminology or jargon used by experts on an issue. Also, there are times when it may be appropriate to ask for the opinions of people who are not familiar with that terminology.

A case in point is the use of the term *impeachment* in polls conducted during the Watergate era. The opinions of those members of the public who were not familiar with the impeachment process were clearly relevant at that time. However, polls that attempted to measure opinion on whether President Nixon should be impeached suffered from a widespread public misapprehension that impeachment meant removal from office. Few understood that impeachment is the first step in the formal process of deciding whether a president should be removed from office, a first step taken by the House of Representatives that is analogous to indictment by a grand jury in criminal proceedings. Because of public confusion, questions such as "Do you think President Nixon should be impeached and compelled to leave office or not?" (asked by the Gallup Poll) and "If the Senate Watergate Committee decides that President Nixon was involved in the coverup, do you think Congress should impeach him or not?" (asked by the Harris Survey) were unable to measure properly the public's opinion as to whether Nixon should be impeached.[55] Eventually, the Gallup Poll developed a question preamble that explained the impeachment process and then followed with the question, "Now let me ask you first of all, if you think there is enough evidence of possible wrongdoing in the case of

President Nixon to bring him to trial before the Senate, or not?" Unless questions are worded to explain technical jargon in everyday language, they cannot be relied on to provide meaningful measures of public opinion.

QUESTIONNAIRE STRUCTURE

The influence that question order exerts on poll results is more pervasive than the illustrations given earlier indicate. A sequence of preceding questions can establish a frame of reference for a question that will bias responses to what would otherwise be an unbiased, balanced question. In preelection polls, for example, in order not to affect the "perceptual environment," most pollsters do not ask any issue questions before they ask for voting intention or preference between candidates.[56] Their concern is that the particular set of questions might give saliency to issues that favor one candidate over the other. This could happen even though each question by itself is fair and unbiased. To see how this can happen, let us consider the questionnaire for a confidential, privately commissioned poll on opinions on Palestinian-Israeli relations.

One question asked, "Who do you think is responsible for the massacre of the Palestinian civilians in the Beirut refugee camps?" Note that the question does not suggest any answers, respondents being free to name whomever comes to their minds. This is a question format specifically designed to obtain unbiased, uninfluenced answers. However, the immediately preceding question was, "Do you favor or oppose the recent Israeli advances on West Beirut?" The wording of that preceding question is, by itself, also unbiased. But, however a respondent answered that question, its wording and position highlighted the fact that Israeli troops were active in the vicinity of the refugee camps, thereby increasing the possibility that Israelis would be named as responsible for the massacre in answer to the subsequent question.

Another question asked, "Today, are your sympathies more with the Israelis or the Palestinians?" Because the order in which answer categories are mentioned can influence responses, in half the interviews Israelis were mentioned first and Palestinians second, and in the other half the order was reversed. This question wording is impeccable when evaluated in isolation. However, the preceding question, which was also the second question in the interview (the first was an innocuous question on how interested the respondent was in following foreign affairs) reads, "Since the Israeli invasion in June, do you think things in the Middle East are going in the right direction, or have they pretty seriously gotten off on the wrong track?" Although the second question in itself is balanced, it does direct attention to a widely criticized military act by Israel. Heightening the saliency of that act by asking about it first increases the likelihood of getting pro-Palestinian rather than pro-Israeli responses to the next question on sympathy.

We must also consider the effect of starting the interview by asking for an evaluation of the Israeli move into Lebanon. That effect could have been drastically changed if the following question had presented the Israeli justification and then asked whether the respondent agreed or disagreed with it. In fact, such a question was ultimately asked, about fifty questions later at the very end of the interview, and only after many questions about agreement or disagreement with pro-Palestinian arguments had been asked. Thus, although the individual questions asked in this poll are beyond criticism, the order in which they were asked created a frame of reference that predisposed respondents to pro-Palestinian answers.

The American Association for Public Opinion Research, a professional association, has developed standards of disclosure when poll results are released. One of the provisions in these standards is that the exact wording of questions be reported. Important as it is to cite exact wordings, it is equally important to know the question sequence. Opinions do not exist in a void. They are imbedded in a context that can be manipulated by question order as much as by question wording.

THE MULTIDIMENSIONALITY OF ISSUES

The context of opinions is normally quite complex. As a result, if a poll covers only one dimension of an issue, only a partial picture of public opinion on that issue can be developed, no matter how many questions are asked about it. An interesting illustration of this principle comes from a poll that I directed for Gallup on behalf of *Newsweek* in November 1970.[57]

That poll investigated public attitudes regarding the American system of law and justice and was conducted at a time when 56 percent of the public said that "reducing the amount of crime" was the most important domestic problem. The survey probed attitudes toward the police, the prosecution of accused, the courts, and the prisons. By asking about all these dimensions of the criminal justice system, the survey revealed a complexity of attitudes that would otherwise have been missed.

When asked to select which of eleven statements they felt represented serious problems, 75 percent selected "Convicted criminals are let off too easily" and 68 percent chose "It takes too long before accused people are brought to trial." The survey also found that "law and order" advocates, such as then Governor Ronald Reagan, were rated much more favorably for their stand on how to treat criminals than were spokespersons for a more liberal approach such as Senator Edward Kennedy. Taken by themselves, these results lead to the conclusion that most of the public had a consistently punitive, "hard-hat" orientation on the crime issue.

Other results indicated that the preceding question encompassed only one dimension of public opinion. Of particular interest are the replies to a series of three questions that asked what should be done to make the police, the courts, and the prisons more effective in reducing crime. For the police, law-and-order answers predominated over non-law-and-order answers by a ratio of 65 percent to 46 percent. For prisons, *non*-law-and-order answers predominated by a ratio of 64 percent to 21 percent. For courts, law-and-order answers were almost equal to non-law-and-order answers by a ratio of 49 percent to 48 percent. These results suggest that although the public strongly favored a hard-line law-and-order policy to ensure safe streets, it was at the same time receptive to a more ameliorative policy in treating convicts while in prison.[58]

The danger of ignoring multidimensionality has been demonstrated by Roll and Cantril, who described how a candidate for a county office was misled by a poll that showed 57 percent were in favor of immediately building a vocational high school with county funds instead of waiting until federal and state funds were available for building both a vocational school and a junior college.[59] A week before election, the candidate proposed an ambitious plan for a complex that would include a new jail and other county buildings as well as the school without considering how cost-consciousness might affect voting decisions. She lost the election, 54 percent to 46 percent, although in an earlier poll she led by a two to one margin. Thus, polls that deal only with one dimension of an issue produce partial and, to that extent, distorted measurements of public opinion.

MOVEMENTS IN OPINION

In order to place public opinion in context, one of the things pollsters must do is chart the movement of opinion in reaction to events.[60] Public opinion is a dynamic process, always reacting to the continuous flow of events. We have already seen how, for example, candidate standings may change (at least temporarily) in reaction to televised debates. Because this process of unending reaction cannot be captured by a single poll, relying on one poll to determine what the public thinks can result in distortion. An in-depth analysis of public opinion

FIGURE 3.1
Approval of USSR and Communism

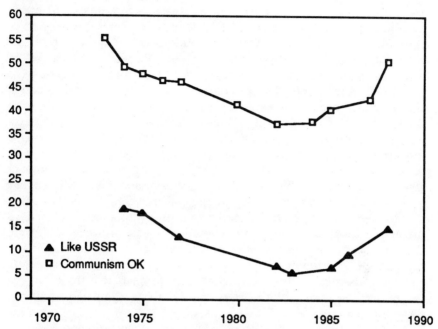

Source: GSS News (National Opinion Research Center) no. 2 (September 1988), p. 3. Used by permission.

requires measurements of trend as much as questions that probe opinions on more than one facet of an issue.

When measuring trends in opinion, we must distinguish between long-term movements and reactions to specific events. The National Opinion Research Center's General Social Survey (GSS) conducts annual surveys that track long-term movement in public opinion on a wide range of issue domains. As shown in Figure 3.1, those surveys have shown how "liking of the USSR and approval of Communism as a form of government fell from the mid-1970s to the early 1980s as detente was replaced by what some some commentators called the 'Second Cold War.' Since 1983–84, however, attitudes towards the Soviet Union and Communism have become more favorable."[61] Such long-term trends are of great value in identifying how the general climate of opinion may be changing. However, an accurate chart of changing public opinion in relation to specific events of political significance depends on fairly frequent measurements. Infrequent, sporadic polls may register an impression of how the public is reacting to events that is false.

Figure 3.2 shows the trend in approval of Lyndon B. Johnson's performance as president, as measured by the Gallup Poll, during 1966–1967.[62] A total of twenty-nine measurements were taken during these critical years, which were marked by a continuing escalation of U.S. military involvement in Vietnam. In addition to what were probably random monthly fluctuations, the trend in Johnson's approval rating was marked by a number of sharp reversals. Particularly dramatic were the plunge in the winter and spring of 1966 as U.S. military participation escalated without any notable successes, the sharp upturn following the beginning of the bombing of North Vietnam, and the equally sharp fall to the previous low as hopes that the bombing would bring a quick end to the conflict were disappointed. A period of minor fluctuations followed, without any real change in opinion. Then, the summer 1967 summit meeting between Lyndon Johnson and Nikita Khrushchev at New Jersey's Glassboro State College was followed by another sharp improvement in Johnson's approval rating. But the outbreak of riots in urban ghettos that summer quickly eroded that improvement. Despite these repeated changes, the long-term trend was clearly downward and marked the continuing deterioration of Johnson's political strength. Annual polls such as the GSS might suffice to chart that trend but not to analyze reaction to the start of the bombing campaign or to the Glassboro meeting.

To demonstrate the pitfalls of relying on a few, sporadic polls to measure the trend of public opinion, let us assume that Gallup had conducted only three polls during the period June 1966–July 1967. Figures 3.3 and 3.4 are each based on that assumption and show the trend as based on two different sets of polls selected from Figure 3.2. Looking at Figure 3.3, we would conclude that Johnson's approval rating was satisfactorily constant for the first part of that period, with almost half approving, and that it then got even better after the Glassboro meeting. Figure 3.4, however, shows a different picture, with the first part of that period marked by a sharp decline and then a substantial, although partial, recovery after the Glassboro meeting. Only with the full trend line as shown in Figure 3.2 is the real movement in public opinion in reaction to the course of the Vietnam conflict discernible.

The trend in Reagan's approval rating during the 1986 Senate hearings on diversion of funds to the contras in Nicaragua and the sale of arms to Iran also requires frequent measures to be properly understood. For months before those hearings his approval rating was stable in a range of 61 percent to 63 percent. It then dropped precipitously to 47 percent in December and 48 percent in January 1987. After a further decline to 40 percent approve in February, Reagan's approval recovered to 46 percent in March. Subsequent monthly polls showed little change

FIGURE 3.2
Approval of Lyndon B. Johnson, 1966–1967

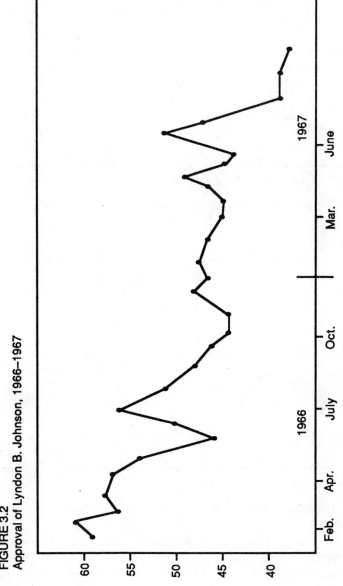

Source: *Gallup Opinion Index*, no. 29 (November 1967), pp. 2–3.

FIGURE 3.3
Approval of Lyndon B. Johnson, Using Selected Polling Dates: I

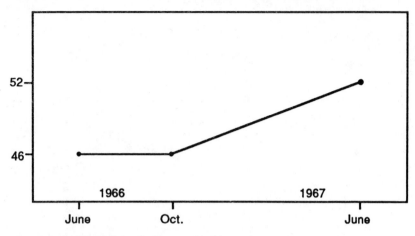

Source: Gallup Opinion Index, no. 29 (November 1967), pp. 2–3.

FIGURE 3.4
Approval of Lyndon B. Johnson, Using Selected Polling Dates: II

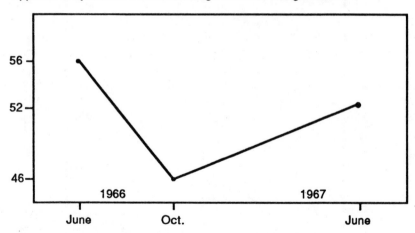

Source: Gallup Opinion Index, no. 29 (November 1967), pp. 2–3.

during the rest of 1987.[63] We might conclude from the extended periods of stability that monthly readings of a president's popularity are fruitless. Only when sudden changes and reversals occur is the value of frequent readings of public opinion evident.

Concentrating on the complexities and dynamics of public opinion, however, does have its pitfalls. The danger is that the ultimate political question—namely, which side does the public favor—may be forgotten. Although public opinion can, and does, experience sharp swings and reversals, a summary measure of the public mood at given points in time is essential for an understanding of the public's thinking on an issue. Examining only the complexities may be as distorting as ignoring them. A sophisticated use of public opinion polls combines both approaches: asking global, summary questions periodically to chart the overall direction of movement of opinion and asking more specific, probing questions to analyze the reasons for that movement. For a full and valid investigation of public opinion, it is necessary to employ a dual strategy that seeks both to measure the direction of opinion change at various points in time and to analyze the processes through which opinion evolves and crystallizes. Anything short of that can only produce a truncated, and to that degree distorted, picture of public opinion. Conducting polls with these dual purposes in mind would increase the possibility that they will provide us with socially useful information about public opinion.

THE NATURE OF PUBLIC OPINION AS MEASURED BY POLLS

The foregoing review of methodological problems has substantive implications regarding the sense in which public opinion polls can and do measure public opinion. At the risk of oversimplification, pollsters can be classified into two groups that are reminiscent of Gallup's and Rogers's contrasting conceptualizations of public opinion (see Chapter 1). One group adopts election day as its model, assuming that opinions can be measured in the same way that voting intentions are measured. The other group conceives of public opinion as a complex, ever-changing process.

When opinions are measured in the same way as voting intentions, the result is a curiously static and usually simplistic picture of public opinion. The tally of responses to a single question, or at the most two or three questions, is treated as if it were public opinion incarnate, a tangible "thing," as it were, whose dimensions have now been determined. The complexities of opinions and their propensity to change are ignored. Instead, attention is focused on the cleavage lines along which opinion has presumably crystallized. When opinion has indeed crystallized, such a picture of public opinion is not necessarily a distortion. In fact, when public opinion has crystallized to the point where the public is ready to act on an issue, polls designed along these lines can provide politically meaningful measurements of public opinion. When the chips are down and the public is mobilized, knowing how the public splits on an issue is pertinent and important. Under those circumstances, a well-designed referendum-type poll can tell us something valid about public opinion.

On the other hand, conducting polls that conform to the election model when public opinion has not crystallized can lead to serious error. The results of such polls are typically presented as quasireferenda or plebiscites through which the "general will" (to use Jean-Jacques Rousseau's term) has somehow been discovered. In fact, no "general will" exists under those conditions, and poll results then verge on the meaningless as a valid measure of public opinion.

Polls based on the contrasting conception of public opinion as a dynamic process focus on the complexity of opinions and their susceptibility to change. Such polls recognize that public thinking on issues seldom falls into neat, consistent, logical patterns. Furthermore, individuals differ as to how well informed they are on various issues, which particular aspects of an issue matter to them, and how intensely committed they are to a particular position. The result is that rather than being crystallized, most of the time on most issues public opinion is relatively amorphous, subject to change, and passive, with only a minority of the public mobilized pro or con. Under those circumstances, polls that investigate public opinion by probing its complexity and dynamics and do not merely ask how many are for or against a specified position are essential for an understanding that is true to reality.

CONCLUSION

We have identified a number of characteristics of public opinion polls that must be considered in any discussion of how, and to what extent, polls can make a positive contribution to the nation's political life. Briefly, those characteristics are:

1. Despite the hopes of the early pollsters, and the fears of their critics, public opinion polls have not played a major role in the setting of public policy. Polls are used extensively by politicians, officeholders, and special interest groups to develop election campaigns and campaigns to promote particular policies—but seldom to formulate policy.
2. Despite the interest of both news media and politicians in preelection polls as predictions of how people will vote, polls—especially those conducted appreciably in advance of an election—have limited value for that purpose. Basing decisions regarding

whom to support solely, or primarily, on candidate standings in early polls is not warranted.

3. The sensitivity of opinion polls to the wording and sequence of questions demonstrates the limited value of using one question, no matter how objective and unbiased its wording, to investigate and analyze public opinion on an issue. When we add in the imprecision inherent in any sample survey, we must conclude that opinion polls cannot and should not be treated as plebiscites on public opinion.

4. Public opinion is a dynamic process that changes in reaction to an ever-changing world. To understand public opinion, we must understand how it responds to events and how those responses generate long-term trends in the climate of opinion. Irregularly conducted "snapshots" of opinion do not give us the information needed for a full understanding of public opinion.

We must also conclude that the early critics of polls were wrong in their belief that polls can never tell us much about public opinion that is meaningful. If polls were an unsatisfactory method for investigating public opinion, politicians and special interest groups would not find information obtained from polls so useful in planning and evaluating their campaigning, lobbying, and public relations activities. That polls do provide useful information to those who seek to mold and manipulate public opinion is as good an indicator as one could want that polls can tell us something meaningful about public opinion.

But those same early critics were correct in their attacks on the tendency of many pollsters to assume that the complexities of public opinion can be satisfactorily summarized in the responses to plebiscitarian, referenda-type questions. By themselves, such questions provide a superficial reading of public opinion that can often be misleading. Because referenda-type questions do not inform us about the sources and dynamics of public opinion, they do not identify what underlies the transient opinions of the day. That failure can lead to an incorrect understanding of the public's thinking on issues.

In light of these observations, we must change the terms of the early debate about polls, even though the issues raised at that time are still significant. Instead of being preoccupied with the possibility that politicians and policymakers will blindly "follow the polls," we ought to be more concerned with the manipulative uses of polls. Although the instrumental use of polls for political intelligence may, and sometimes does, sensitize politicians and policymakers to the public's concerns, we cannot assume that this will necessarily follow.

If public opinion polls are to further the responsiveness of political leaders without a resultant sacrifice of their individual responsibility, two conditions must be met. First, sophisticated polling methods must be employed. Our review of polling methods in this chapter has suggested directions for development. Second, existing means for introducing the results of sophisticated polls into public debate must be strengthened, and even more effective mechanisms than are now available must be developed. We turn to this second consideration in the next chapter.

4

POLLS, NEWS MEDIA, AND PUBLIC DEBATE

We began our examination of public opinion polls by contending that because polls have become an integral part of U.S. political life, rather than debating whether we should pay any attention to them, we should concern ourselves with the purposes to which polls are put. We then turned our attention to methodological considerations that affect the validity of how polls are used. Yet we cannot simply ignore the view that polls, by their very nature, sap democratic government, and that it is futile to attempt using them to further democracy. Because polls will undoubtedly remain part of the political scene in the foreseeable future and because they are widely used to manipulate the public, we shall focus our attention on identifying what must be done if polls are to have a constructive effect. We must ask whether we can identify conditions in which polls can make a positive contribution to democratic governance or whether they must be written off as inherently pernicious. As we shall see, the role of the news media in polling and in fostering public debate is of decisive significance in this regard.

The view that polls are detrimental to our political life is not restricted to the theoretical writings of social philosophers and social scientists. Many successful politicians also take this position, often in harshly critical terms.

Leadership by polls is weak, uninspired, uninformed, not innovative, and contributes only to temporary success. There is a tendency for politicians or elected officials to tell the people what the polls show and the public wants to hear (unnamed governor of a Midwestern state).

Is there a danger that polls have become a dangerous element in our electoral process in recent years, influencing elections rather than offering insights into voter sentiment on candidates and issues (unnamed senator from an Eastern state)?[1]

Criticisms such as these are to a considerable degree warranted. All too often, unthinking, uninformed users of polls have misinterpreted and overinterpreted poll results. Particularly deleterious has been the proclivity to assume that adding up the answers to individual poll questions provides us with all we need to know about public opinion. Nonetheless, even the harshest poll critics do not question the need of leaders in a democracy to know, although not automatically to conform to, the public's opinion regarding the issues of the day. Our concern is whether polls can be used to fulfill that need in a constructive way.

In populous, highly organized societies, institutional channels of communications are not up to the task of keeping national leaders informed about the thoughts, feelings, and wishes of the general population. The very inchoateness of these psychological phenomena make them inaccessible unless special means of tapping them are instituted. Only under extraordinary circumstances—for example, public reaction to the "Saturday night massacre" during the Watergate investigations (when Attorney-General Elliot Richardson and Deputy Attorney-General William Ruckelshaus both resigned rather than fire special investigator Archibald Cox)—does public reaction mobilize so clearly that no special effort has to be made to discover what the public feels. But those are crisis circumstances in which public reactions can be politically destabilizing. As Benjamin Ginsberg has observed, "Through the nineteenth century, public opinion was usually equated with riots, strikes, demonstrations, and boycotts."[2] Stable governments need to know about the public's thinking and cannot afford to wait for the spontaneous mobilization of public opinion in crisis.

ISSUES IN REPORTING POLL RESULTS

Before the invention of polling, authoritarian governments (such as Napoleon's France, Hitler's Germany, and Stalin's Soviet Union) relied on subjective observations by secret agents to keep track of potentially dangerous movements in public psychology. Democratic societies, on the other hand, rely on periodic elections to maintain a stable relation between government and public opinion. For many purposes, that suffices. But, the periods between elections are often characterized by developments that make election results outdated, thereby weakening the linkage between the public and political leaders.

Traditional channels of communication during periods between elections include the lobbying efforts of organized interest groups, direct contact with elected representatives such as the proverbial "letter to your Congressman," and letters to newspapers. Nevertheless, access to and utilization of such channels tends to be limited to a small segment of the public. Moreover, the leaderships of organized interest groups, especially those with mass memberships, may themselves be out of touch with rank-and-file opinion or else have agendas of their own. The result is that the opinions of many are not heard by their representatives and do not enter public debate and legislative deliberations. The danger in those circumstances is not that political leaders will not conform to public opinion but that they will not take into account and consider the concerns, wants, and aspirations of the entire public.

It is precisely under those conditions that public opinion polls could perform their most useful function in a democracy—namely, ensuring that debate on public issues in periods between elections will not ignore public opinion. This function can be performed only if poll results are widely disseminated and do not become privileged information to which only political elites have access. For poll results to enrich public debates, however, they must not only become public property; they must be reported to the public in ways that are appropriate and meaningful.

Reporting Polls as Elections

Elections are widely and inappropriately used as a model for public opinion polls. This has an unfortunate effect on the way poll results are reported in the news media because the key question in reporting election results—Who won?—is inevitably adopted as the model on which to peg all poll reports. In some cases, such as polls on the electorate's response to debates between candidates, considerable effort, time, and money are expended on identifying the "winner," but on little else. As with the race on election night to be first with the news as to who has won the election, there is a race to announce who has won the debate. One-half hour after the first Bush-Dukakis debate in 1988, ABC News anchor Peter Jennings interrupted that network's postdebate commentary to announce the results of interviews with a national sample of some 500 viewers who were asked which candidate they thought had "won" that debate.[3] That poll and others that sought to determine who won (most notably polls conducted by the *Los Angeles Times,* by Gallup for *Newsweek,* and by CBS News/*New York Times*) were widely disseminated by the Associated Press and were typically given front-page treatment.[4]

There are two aspects to the news coverage of postdebate polls that are relevant here. One is the stress on the figures as to who "won"— according to ABC News Dukakis won by 44 percent to Bush's 36 percent, whereas the other polls had it a virtual tie (*Los Angeles Times:* Dukakis 35 percent, Bush 34 percent; Gallup/*Newsweek:* Dukakis 42 percent, Bush 41 percent; CBS News/*New York Times:* Bush 42 percent, Dukakis 39 percent)—just as if an election had been held. The results of postdebate poll questions about perceived qualities of the candidates received secondary treatment or were ignored. Second is the reporting of interviews with "expert" political analysts and spokespersons for the two candidates who interpreted the political meaning of those figures.[5] The poll results were treated more as news events, as if they were election results, than as expressions of public opinion, with the underlying public opinion left to the speculative, subjective commentary of experts and political manipulators (an ironic contrast to the expectation of early pollsters that polling would replace subjective interpretation). When polls are reported in this way, they do not tell us much about public opinion and cannot possibly play a constructive, democratizing role.

When poll reports on issues are modeled after elections, a comparably negative effect occurs. Ironically, more often than not, such polls turn out to be politically irrelevant. A case in point are three questions dealing with proposed gun control legislation asked by the Gallup Poll at the height of the 1988 presidential campaign:[6]

- "Would you favor or oppose a national law requiring a 7-day waiting period before a handgun could be purchased, in order to determine whether the prospective buyer has been convicted of a felony or is mentally ill?"
- "Do you favor or oppose the registration of all firearms?"
- "Would you favor or oppose a law requiring that any person who carries a gun outside his home must have a license to do so?"

Support for all three proposals was overwhelming: 91 percent favored the seven-day waiting period, 67 percent favored the registration of all firearms (58 percent of gun owners expressed approval), and 84 percent favored requiring a license to carry a gun outside the home.

As noted in the release reporting these results, Dukakis favored strict gun control laws while Bush opposed them. Considering the one-sidedness of the poll results, we might expect that gun control would have been a strong issue working in Dukakis's favor. Yet, not only did Bush decisively defeat Dukakis; other poll data suggested that by tying gun control to a soft-on-crime theme, Bush was able to use this issue to his advantage. When polls are treated as pseudo-plebiscites, presumably telling the nation's political leaders what to do without casting much light on the workings of public thinking on an issue—the goals that the public wants to achieve, why it has those goals, and what it thinks are good ways of achieving them—they are more likely to weaken than strengthen meaningful public debate.

Methodological Issues in Poll Reporting

The often simplistic questions and analytical methods that were common in the early years of polling, and that still characterize too many public opinion polls, are legitimate targets of criticism. However, at its best, poll methodology has evolved far beyond the simplistic techniques that were once the norm. Pollsters have developed a variety of questioning techniques for probing the many facets of public opinion and now pay more attention to tracing how opinions change over time instead of relying on one-time measurements. To counteract the proclivity of many to think of the public as a monolithic entity, sophisticated poll analysts have learned to examine the public's heterogeneity and diversity of opinion.

Question styles

If current state-of-the-art methods are used, polls can be reported not as plebiscites but as probings into the dynamics of public opinion. A poll conducted by the *Los Angeles Times*[7] that investigated the potential political significance of presidential hopeful Pat Robertson illustrates what can be done when innovative questions are asked. Three separate series of questions were asked in this poll. When the responses to all three are examined together, they document the difficult barriers that Pat Robertson faced before he could hope to achieve nomination, let alone election.

One series of questions in that poll asked about abortion, homosexuality, pornography, school prayer, and the proposed Equal Rights Amendment—all issues that were of particular concern to religious fundamentalists, who constituted Robertson's core supporters. Nationally, opinions varied on these issues, with a majority favoring the conservative side in some instances, a fairly even split on others, and a decided majority on the liberal side in others. As to be expected, white fundamentalists were more conservative on all these issues than was the rest of the public, but in some cases not so decisively as might be expected. For example, a sizable proportion of white fundamentalists (43 percent) favored an Equal Rights Amendment. Thus, we could reasonably infer that basing his candidacy exclusively on these issues would not in itself generate support for Robertson among a majority of the total electorate who were more liberal on these issues than white fundamentalists were.

A second series asked whether the respondent would be more likely or less likely to vote for a "political candidate who described himself as an evangelical Christian." In this instance, the public at large said it would be *less* likely to vote for such a candidate, by a two and one-half to one ratio. Only among white fundamentalists, a minority of the total electorate, was the weight of opinion in favor of an evangelical Christian, by three to one. The overall political effect of being identified as an evangelical Christian, therefore, was more likely to be negative than positive.

A third series of questions dealt more closely with Pat Robertson's candidacy, although without mentioning his name. The people interviewed were read word pictures of two possible candidates for the presidency—their marital status, number of children, ages, occupations, and place of birth—and then were asked which one they would like to see as president. In half the interviews one of the candidates was described as a Protestant minister and in the other half he was not. In all other ways the two word pictures were identical. The hypothetical candidate lost by 57 percent to 23 percent when he was described as a Protestant minister, compared to a much narrower margin of 40 percent to 35 percent when he was not. Even among white fundamentalists, adding the identification of Protestant minister cost the fictional candidate ten percentage points.

Two aspects of this approach to investigating public opinion regarding a Pat Robertson candidacy should be emphasized. First, the poll was not the typical trial heat asking whether a person would vote for Robertson. Instead, the poll probed the assumptions underlying a putative Robertson candidacy. Second, the poll did not predict that Robertson could not win; rather, it suggested that being an evangelical minister was more of a handicap than an asset for an aspiring presidential candidate.

Analytical techniques

Analytical techniques exist to go beyond mere measurement of the public's overall opinion on specific issues. At a minimum, techniques are available for examining the extent to which a particular opinion is associated with the respondent's socioeconomic, political, and personal characteristics as well as with opinions on other issues. Whereas some of these techniques require sophisticated statistical models, others are straightforward but potentially incisive ways of analyzing the dynamics of public opinion. That these techniques are not beyond the capabilities of public opinion polls is demonstrated by the fact that upon occasion they have been used.

For example, a CBS/*New York Times* poll conducted in the period between the 1988 Democratic and Republican nominating conventions when Dukakis was supported by 47 percent to Bush's 39 percent went beyond measuring voting preferences. A series of questions asked (1) for an overall opinion of Bush and Dukakis; (2) whether each candidate says what he thinks; (3) confidence in each candidate during a difficult international crisis; (4) who would be more competent in managing the federal government; and (5) who would be more likely to raise taxes. In reporting the results of these questions the *Times* examined the responses of two key segments of the electorate—those who were "undecided" at the time and "Reagan Democrats" (those who said they had voted for Reagan in 1984 even though they considered themselves Democrats).[8] This analysis identified the inroads Dukakis was making among Reagan Democrats, some of which he retained on Election Day, and Bush's early strength on tax increases and on handling foreign crises among these swing voters.

Another example is an October 1988 Gallup Poll that reported that the proportion of the electorate that felt that they are "financially better off now than [they] were a year ago" and also thought that "at this time next year [they] will be financially better off than now" had risen from 31 percent in September 1984 to 44 percent in September 1988.[9] This overall composite measurement was further analyzed by party identification, comparing the incidence of what Gallup called "superoptimists" among self-identified Democrats, Independents, and Republicans. Gallup found that among Democrats the proportion of these "superoptimists" had doubled from 17 percent in 1984 to 34 percent in 1988. Among Independents, the increase was from 32 percent to 47 percent. This optimistic perception of economic trends among those segments of the public that Dukakis had to attract if he were to win the 1988 presidential election was a significant part of the context of his eventual defeat.

Similar cross-analyses can uncover complexities and even seeming contradictions in public opinion that are often ignored. An analysis of a March 1988 CBS News/*New York Times* poll revealed, for example, that "even among those who approve of President Reagan's performance in office, only 50 percent said the Administration has made a serious effort against drugs. . . . 42 percent said it had not." In that same survey, self-described conservatives and Republicans felt, by a margin of better than two to one, that it was more important to stop the drug dealings of anti-Communist leaders in Central America than to support those leaders because they were anti-Communists.[10] That is to say, even among those segments of the public for whom fighting Communist incursions had a very high priority, fighting drugs had an even higher priority. This type of analysis gives an insight into public concern about drugs that could not be achieved simply by reporting that among all those interviewed in that poll, 63 percent chose putting an end to drug dealing as more important, while 21 percent said stopping communism was.

During the 1988 presidential election campaign, the Times-Mirror, publisher of the *Los Angeles Times*, used a *psychographic* technique to analyze opinions and candidate preferences. This technique requires asking a number of questions to classify people according to their attitudes and values rather than their demographic characteristics.[11] Opinions on issues were then analyzed by these classifications to see how people with different psychographics differed in their opinions on issues. In the Times-Mirror study, groupings such as "enterprisers," "moralists," "upbeats," "disaffecteds," "partisan poor," and "God and country Democrats" were compared to see the extent to which they differed in thinking that Bush or Dukakis "is more able to create good economic conditions for people like me." This comparison was done separately for men and women, and revealed that women were more likely to name Dukakis than were men who shared similar attitudes and values.

All the preceding examples of the analytic use of polls occurred during election campaigns, when the news media are relatively amenable to allocating some resources to analyzing voter preferences. Even during election campaigns, simple horse-race polls continue to predominate. Willingness to use more sophisticated ways of measuring and analyzing public opinion is even rarer when polls are conducted on issues and not on candidate standings.

Analyzing issues

An illustration of how polls can be used to analyze public opinion on issues outside the context of an election is a series of four surveys conducted by The Roper Organization for the United States Olympic Committee (USOC). These surveys measured public reaction to President Carter's call for a boycott of the 1980 Moscow summer Olympics as a way of protesting the Soviet invasion of Afghanistan. Majority support for a boycott was registered in the first poll, conducted in

January 1980, and persisted with little change in the three subsequent polls, the last conducted in April after the USOC had agreed not to participate in the summer games.[12] Thus, at the simplest level of description, we must conclude that Carter's call for a boycott received the public's solid endorsement, but that conclusion tells us nothing about the reason for the endorsement.

These surveys also asked whether the games should be moved to another site, whether the United States should boycott the games under a number of different circumstances, and whether a variety of arguments for and against a boycott provided strong reasons for each position. Additional questions dealt with interest in and reaction to U.S. participation in the 1980 winter games, especially the U.S. hockey team's upset victory over the Soviet Union's team in the 1980 winter Olympics, and knowledge about the USOC.

An analysis of the answers to the entire series of questions revealed that support for a boycott was based on its symbolic significance, not on the expectation that a boycott would influence Soviet behavior. A rally-round-the-president response was also evident in the poll results. In fact, even those who professed commitment to the principle that the Olympics should be politically neutral did not oppose the boycott.

As used by the USOC, the four polls did not serve as a plebiscite, instructions from the public, as it were, to the USOC as to what it should do. Instead, by providing an insight into why the public supported a boycott and what it expected a boycott to achieve, those polls enabled the USOC to take the public's thinking into account before deciding what to do and how to announce its decision.

THE CONTRIBUTION OF POLLS TO PUBLIC DEBATE

The USOC's use of polls contrasts with the League of Women Voters' decision that whether it would invite John Anderson, running on a third-party ticket, to participate in the 1980 presidential debates would depend upon his standing in preelection polls. In turning to polls for guidance, the League assumed that candidate standings in preelection polls provided a sufficient basis for determining whether someone was a major candidate. The League did not use polls to investigate and analyze the public's thinking on what constitutes a major candidate and what criteria are relevant when deciding whom to invite. The latter kind of analysis would have provided useful input to the League's decision without making poll results the determining criterion. Thus, even though the League's intent was to adhere to the principle that deciding whom to invite was a responsibility it should not shirk, it ended up abdicating its authority to "the polls."

On the other hand, the results of the four polls commissioned by the USOC were reported privately to it and were not made public until a year later—and then in an unpublicized talk given to a professional association. Although the polls were of value to the USOC, they did not enter into the extended public debate as to whether the USOC should abide by Carter's call for a boycott. In contrast, the League of Women Voters made public its decision to rely on candidate standings in the polls when determining whether to invite John Anderson to participate in the debates. Making their decison public resulted in its becoming a matter of public debate. So long as poll results are privileged information, to be used by private groups and not subject to public debate, whether they will be used manipulatively or not will depend upon the inclinations of whoever sponsors the poll. If poll results are released, however, they become fair game for criticism and public debate. The likelihood that poll results can be successfully used for manipulative purposes is then reduced.

A case in point is a 1969 poll (mentioned in Chapter 2) conducted during the height of Senate debate over the Safeguard ABM system. A group calling itself Citizens Committee for Peace with Security took full-page advertisements in leading newspapers reporting the poll's results under the headline "84% of all Americans Support an ABM System." After protracted protests by some opinion research practitioners that the advertisement distorted the poll results, the full question wording, including a prefatory statement to the question, and the sequence of preceding questions was released. This information made it obvious to any professional, and probably to any objective layperson, that the wording and sequence were strongly biased to elicit a pro-ABM response. The firm that had conducted the survey then repudiated the interpretation of the poll results that had been presented in the advertisement.[13] If the poll results had not been publicized but, as is commonly done, circulated privately to influential senators and representatives, it is very unlikely that the interpretation of the poll results made by the pro-Safeguard group would have become a matter of public debate and would ultimately have been repudiated.

Increasing the Range of Public Debate

When publicly released poll results do no more than measure the split in pro-con sentiment on an issue, public debate about them is likely to center on the objectivity or bias of the question rather than on the public's thinking on the issue. The more analytical a poll is, however, the more possible it is that debate will go beyond methodology to a consideration of what can be learned about public opinion from a poll. In 1968, for example, when polls revealed that part of George Wallace's support came from people who were doves on Vietnam, startled political analysts began to reconsider their assumptions about who Wallace's supporters were. However, those same polls did no more than measure candidate preferences and therefore provided no explanation for this unexpected finding.

Light on why some of Wallace's support came from doves is cast by a reanalysis of two questions asked on a 1969 poll conducted by The Gallup Organization for *Newsweek*.[14] One question asked about the moral justification for U.S. involvement in the Vietnam conflict, whereas the other asked about the moral justification for demands then being made by black leaders. This analysis showed that there was little correlation between "liberal" or "conservative" responses to the two questions. For example, those who felt "we had no right or reason to send our troops to fight in Vietnam" tended to be more negative than the rest of the sample regarding the moral justification for black demands. Those who felt "it was our right and duty to send our troops to fight the Communists" split on whether black leaders were justified in their demands in the same proportions as did the total sample. No consistently conservative or liberal response to these questions existed among Republicans, Democrats, or Independents. This would explain why it was so difficult at that time for either hawks or doves to forge effective political coalitions that could speak for a majority.

That poll also found that 49 percent of those interviewed endorsed intermediate positions regarding the justification for U.S. presence in Vietnam. In other words, in opposition to common stereotypes, the public was not split into a conservative, hawkish, anti–civil rights segment versus a liberal, dovish, pro–civil rights segment. Instead, the public expressed a kaleidoscope of opinions on civil rights and Vietnam, and the dominant opinion on Vietnam was intermediate between hawk and dove.

If, at the time, the public and its leaders had had an accurate perception of public opinion regarding Vietnam, that might have directed public debate away from the polar views of hawks and doves toward intermediate alternatives more acceptable to the majority. Such a turn in public debate might have helped moderate political leaders put together a majority for a Vietnam policy other than the diametrically opposed alternatives of military victory or complete and immediate withdrawal that were the focus of public debate. As Hadley Cantril has shown, our perceptions of what the world is like—what he termed our "reality worlds"—shape and direct our behavior.[15] The misperception that the public was sharply split between two irreconcilable groups—conservative anti–civil rights hawks and liberal pro–civil rights doves—undoubtedly contributed to the bitterness of public debate. Furthermore, that misperception undoubtedly limited the policy choices that moderate leaders thought were politically feasible.

Whether more incisive, analytical polling on Vietnam would have, in fact, helped forge an effective moderate majority, thereby lessening the bitterness and hatred that characterized the Vietnam era, is a moot point. As early as 1966, a group of social scientists privately sponsored an intensive poll that indicated that the public was more receptive to a conciliatory policy leading to negotiations than was generally realized.[16] Despite the professional credentials of the sponsors of the poll and the organization that conducted it (NORC), it could not escape the onus that the sponsoring group was publicly identified as favoring a less bellicose policy. The poll was treated by the news media more as an advocacy poll than as an objective measurement of public opinion. This may be one important reason it had little influence on the course of public debate.

In any event, the intensity of dove and hawk commitment to their respective positions swamped the preferences of the moderate majority. It is not sufficient for a particular policy to be favored by a majority. Political leaders must believe that the majority truly favors that policy and must then be prepared to pay attention to that majority. That is unlikely to happen unless they accept the credentials of a poll as a disinterested measurement of public opinion, provided political leaders are ready to accept any poll results as basic terms for public debate.

Similar considerations apply to such continuing, emotion-laden issues as abortion. Over the years, polls have consistently shown that most citizens oppose a constitutional ban on abortion. For example, a 1982 CBS News/*New York Times* poll found that only 28 percent of a national sample felt that a woman should be forbidden to have an abortion during the first three months of pregnancy.[17] In five polls conducted during the five-year period from 1975 to 1981, the Gallup Poll asked whether abortion should be legal. In all five polls, with virtually no fluctuation from year to year, slightly more than one-half said that abortion should be legal only under certain circumstances, just over one-fifth felt that abortion should be legal under any circumstances, and about one-fifth felt that it should be illegal in all circumstances.[18]

Aiding the Development of Majority-Endorsed Policy

A CBS News/*New York Times* Poll conducted in January 1989, when attention was turning to the possibility that a new, more conservative

Supreme Court might overturn the 1973 *Roe vs. Wade* decision that made abortion a constitutional right, revealed continued majority endorsement of that decision: 61 percent agreed that "if a woman wants to have an abortion and her doctor agrees to it, she should be allowed to have an abortion." In that same poll, 46 percent felt that abortion should be legal as it is now; another 41 percent felt that abortion should be legal but only in cases such as rape, incest, or to save the life of the mother; and only 9 percent said abortion should not be permitted at all.[19]

Reporting the foregoing poll results by themselves does not contribute to an understanding of public opinion on abortion that would enrich public debate. A deeper probing and analysis of opinion are necessary for such an enrichment. The 1981 Gallup Poll, in which 21 percent said that abortion should never be legal, also asked about support for the 1973 Supreme Court decision that, as worded in the question, "a woman may go to a doctor to end pregnancy at any time during the first three months of pregnancy." Forty-five percent favored the Court decision and 46 percent opposed it. Furthermore, in that same survey, a bare 51 percent majority opposed a law that would "declare human life begins at pregnancy and, therefore, abortion at any time could be considered a crime of murder."[20] Clearly, public opinion on abortion is much more than a matter of opposing or favoring it.

A series of questions asked in a December 1977 Gallup Poll casts considerable light on the complexity of public thinking about abortion.[21] The series was asked of those (55 percent of the total sample) who said that abortion should be legal only under certain circumstances. Those people were presented with a list of six circumstances: if the woman's life were endangered, if pregnancy were the result of rape or incest, if the woman would suffer physical damage, if the baby might be born deformed, if the woman's mental health would be endangered, and if she could not afford to have the child. Approval of the legality of abortion under each of these circumstances was then measured separately for the first, second, and third trimesters.

Among those who gave conditional approval to the legality of abortion, the percent that thought abortion should be legal differed drastically depending upon the circumstances. Seventy-seven percent approved the legality of abortion during the first trimester if the woman's life were endangered, compared with 6 percent approval during the third trimester if she could not afford the child. As these results demonstrate, going beyond simple measurements of how many are for or against legal abortion to an analysis of the considerations that affect how people think on this issue is essential for understanding public opinion. Polls that attempt such analyses would enrich public debate and might contribute to the development of a public policy that would achieve majority endorsement. The unfortunate reality is that analytical polls such as this have received little attention in public debate; instead, plebiscitarian "for-or-against" polls have dominated.

It would be foolish to assume that an acceptable public policy on abortion could be forged if only more analytical polls were conducted. Committed "free choice" and "pro-life" adherents cannot be expected to change their views merely because a poll showed that they were in the minority. John Tomicki, executive director of the New Jersey Right to Life Committee, commenting on an April 1989 *Newark Star Ledger*/Eagleton Institute poll that reported that almost seven out of every ten New Jerseyites approved the *Roe vs. Wade* decision, said "even if 90% of the public truly supported abortion, we would still say it's wrong."[22] But the possibility of developing a policy that would be acceptable to most Americans would be enhanced if public debate focused on the circumstances surrounding pregnancy, not on the diametrically opposed positions of the committed extremes. Giving saliency to polls that ask probing questions such as the Gallup series, rather than poll reports that do no more than measure the split of opinion, could help give public debate that focus.

Those few analytical polls on abortion that have been conducted consistently indicate that public debate would be most constructive if it were to focus on the conditions under which abortion should be available and not on whether it should be. Thus, when the results of the 1977 Gallup series are compared with those from the March 1989 *Los Angeles Times* poll cited in Chapter 3, it becomes evident that most of the public has serious reservations about providing unrestricted access to abortion at the same time that it rejects the contention that abortion should be made illegal. It is therefore not surprising that a CBS News/*New York Times* poll conducted one month after the June 1989 Supreme Court decision that invited state governments to impose restrictions on abortion with overturning *Roe vs. Wade* found that "most Americans favor some new legal restrictions on abortion but remain generally wary of government interference with a woman's decision on the matter and regard advocates on one side or the other as 'extremists.'" By a sizable majority of 68 percent, the public felt that "even in cases where they might think abortion is wrong, the government has no business preventing a woman from having an abortion."[23] But 71 percent favored a law that girls under eighteen get parental consent before they could have an abortion, and 60 percent favored "mandatory tests to determine if a fetus could live outside the mother's womb." On the other hand, a minority of 35 percent favored prohibiting public employees and public hospitals from performing abortions while a 52 percent majority opposed such a ban. Simplistic, plebiscitarian polls that ask only whether one favors or opposes a constitution ban on abortion turn attention away from the aspects of the issue that most trouble the public and that are, it follows, most in need of public debate.

Supporting Consensual Politics

That polls often find that much of the public endorses a moderate position rather than any proposed by committed activists has been deplored by some. They contend that "Polls, in effect submerge individuals with strongly held views in a more apathetic mass. The data reported by polls are likely to suggest to public officials that they are working in a more permissive climate of opinion than might have been thought on the basis of alternative indicators of the public mood."[24] But it is exactly the room to maneuver that is needed in legislative deliberations, maneuvers that extremist activists seek to block. If public debate is to be monopolized by those who want no compromise, the strong likelihood is that overt conflict and violence will erupt—as happened during the debate about Vietnam in the 1960s and about abortion in the 1980s.

In the opposition between consensual and confrontational politics, polls unquestionably weigh in on the side of consensus. In that weighing in, plebiscitarian polls enhance the ability of manipulative politicians to further their self-interest and ignore the substantive complexities of issues. On the other hand, polls that seek to understand public opinion can enrich public debate in a way that can be used constructively by innovative leaders. Moreover, analytical polls that reveal the heterogeneity of public opinion can give voice to the needs of subpublics that are usually ignored. When that happens, the possibility that public debate will deal with the concerns of all members of the public and not only the concerns of the powerful will be enhanced.

THE ROLE OF THE NEWS MEDIA

Whether polls will enrich public debate ultimately depends on making their results known to the public in an effective manner. The obvious channel for introducing the results of analytical public opinion polls into public debate is the news media. If only privately commissioned polls were conducted—by candidates for office or by special interest groups as an aid to developing campaign and lobbying strategies—this would severely limit the contribution of polls to public debate. There is nothing inherently wrong in candidates' and special interest groups' using polls in their efforts to convert the public to their point of view—that is part of the constitutional right to freedom of speech. But by themselves such polls contribute more to public manipulation than to the public good.

Opinion polls commissioned by government agencies can add to the responsiveness of policymakers. But the suspicion would always exist that the poll was designed to further the policy goals and partisan interests of the incumbent administration, not to objectively investigate public opinion. Procedures for protecting the credibility of a poll's objectivity would be essential, and even then the possibility that the poll would become the subject of partisan controversy would be great. A public debate on the poll's methodology would be inevitable and, while desirable, would in all likelihood swamp its substantive findings.

Academic survey research institutes periodically conduct polls of public opinion. However, with a few outstanding exceptions such as the Eagleton Institute at Rutgers University, those polls do not poll opinions with sufficient frequency nor are the results reported soon enough for them to make a timely contribution to public debate.

One of the major functions of the news media has always been to keep the public informed about public debate on political issues as well as on events of the day. The news media have long accepted Gallup's original program that polls on the public's views should be reported as news. In accord with that acceptance, the news media have been one of the most important—possibly the most important— sources of financial support for public (as distinct from confidential) opinion polls. Reporting the results of polls conducted for public service and special interest groups as well as academic studies based on surveys on social and economic concerns has also become part of the normal activities of the news media. All this notwithstanding, the performance of the news media in reporting poll results has, with some exceptions, been inadequate to the need.

The preoccupation of the news media with predicting elections has shaped the substance and reporting of media-sponsored polls. During the four-month period September 1987 through January 1988, which was well before the January Iowa caucuses and the February New Hampshire primaries, there were at least 113 published horse-race polls on the Republican candidates and 123 on the Democratic candidates.[25] Karlyn Keene, managing editor of the magazine *Public Opinion,* reported receiving reports of more than 160 published horse-race polls on the presidential contest conducted during the 1988 fall election campaign.[26] This volume of horse-race polling cannot contribute much to our understanding of public opinion. Media polling on nonelection topics has been much less frequent, and the reporting on them has also contributed comparatively little.

Polls as Hard News

Before we can understand why the news media have performed poorly in reporting poll results, we must consider the nature of U.S. journalism. As Roshco has observed, the dominant perspective in U.S. journalism is that news has to do with specific events that have just become known, that are relevant to the public's current interests and concerns, but that are still unknown or only partially known to the public.[27] In accord with that perspective, news reporting focuses on getting that just-acquired information about those interesting events out to the public as soon as possible. The journalist's primary task is to report verified information about those events, not to conduct an analysis that reveals their historical meaning or significance. Furthermore, to attract an audience, events must not only be reported in a timely manner; they must have dramatic content and relate to settings and people that are close to home or, at least, familiar.[28] This is why disasters, violence, conflict, and crises make front-page news, and human interest stories are always welcomed by news editors. This understanding of news defines the "hard news" that constitutes the bulk of what is reported daily by newspapers, television, and radio and conditions how polls are reported by the news media.

A balanced evaluation of how polls are reported must start with an acknowledgement of the number of ways in which polling has benefited from its close ties to journalism.[29] These include (1) the high value placed on factual documentation in hard-news reporting as opposed to editorializing and (2) an interest in public opinion in relation to concrete issues and ongoing events rather than as an abstraction. The objectivity of media-sponsored polls and their relevance to the real world of politics have been enhanced as a result. Nonetheless, in other ways journalistic practices and considerations have created barriers that must be overcome before the news media can fulfill their potential for reporting polls in ways that enrich public debate.

The practice of reporting poll results as hard news creates a major barrier that needs to be overcome if polls are to enrich public debate. Typical of this practice are reports on candidate standings.

Senator Paul Simon has emerged as the clear leader in Iowa in the contest for the Democratic Presidential nomination, according to a new poll that was made public today. . . . It also measured a leveling-off in support for Representative Richard A. Gephardt of Missouri. Mr. Gephardt, who had led the Democratic field in a Register poll released in September, fell to third place in the new survey.[30]

Gary Hart has joined the Rev. Jesse Jackson at the front of the Democratic Presidential field in the latest New York *Times*/CBS News Poll. But Tuesday's survey also found that Mr. Hart has lost more than a third of his support since he withdrew from the contest last May and is rated unfavorably by a substantial minority of Democrats.[31]

In both these reports poll results are presented as the product of an event—the "event" being the poll. This accords with the traditional concept of news as happenings that are important and/or interesting to the public. Because public opinion is not an event but a quality of the polity, in order to qualify as "news," poll reports feature the fact that a poll has been conducted.

In the context of covering developments in an election campaign, with a flow of polls tracking changes in candidate standings, reporting those standings as hard news is not unexpected. The same might also be said about polls designed to measure public reactions to events, such as President Reagan's dispatch of U.S. naval vessels to the Persian Gulf and Gary Hart's decision to withdraw from the race for the Democratic nomination for president.

The American public strongly endorses President Reagan's decision to keep a military presence in the Persian Gulf and supports the use of force to ensure an adequate supply of Middle Eastern oil, a Washington *Post*–ABC News poll indicates.[32]

By 2 to 1, Americans say Gary Hart should not have given up his presidential race, the Los Angeles *Times* Poll has found. But it is also clear from other things they say that Hart probably made a wise decision in getting out.[33]

However justified the hard-news format may be for reporting such polls, the format tends to be a straightjacket into which all poll stories are fitted. As a consequence, polls on long-term issues and problems are equally likely to be reported in a hard-news format:

In the event Admiral John Poindexter and Lt. Col. Oliver North stand trial for their involvement in the Iran-contra affair, 42% of Americans surveyed think Poindexter will be found guilty, while 30% predict this fate for North. Should either man be convicted, the public is more likely to say that North will be given a pardon (51%) than believe this will happen to Poindexter (41%).[34]

After being exposed to most of the key provisions likely to be contained in a final bill, an overwhelming 77–17 percent majority of the American people favor passage of tax reform legislation this year.[35]

The American public, acknowledging that it knows little about the Senate tax bill, remains unconvinced that the bill would produce a fairer tax system or cut many people's taxes, a New York *Times*/CBS News Poll shows. Only 11 percent . . . said they expected to pay lower taxes if the bill became law.[36]

A hard-news format comes naturally to the daily press, geared as it is to reporting the news of the day. Furthermore, newspaper readers and television news viewers expect this format in news stories. And, it can be argued, the news story is in fact about an event—the taking of a poll—and not an analysis of public opinion. Be that as it may, the natural consequence of reporting polls in this manner is to concentrate attention on the numbers that summarize how people answered the poll and to neglect the meaning of those numbers. This practice makes public opinion appear to be a "thing" to be reported rather than a *process* to be analyzed.

The reification of poll results reinforces inclinations to treat the replies to any one question, or series of questions, as if those replies were public opinion incarnate rather than a measure of some aspect(s) of public thinking. If 62 percent of a representative national sample tells the Gallup Poll that it is very important "for the United States and the Soviet Union to sign an arms control agreement within the next few years,"[37] that in itself is not public opinion but a bit of information *about* one aspect of public opinion.

We should not devalue factual reporting of results in covering opinion polls. Documentation is integral to responsible journalism and essential to a valid interpretation of the meaning of poll results. But if only bare-bone percentages are reported, this creates an impression of public opinion as a static thing that is fully represented in those percentages. This impression accounts for the fact that when apparently contradictory results are reported by competing polls that have asked different questions, the cry goes up, "Which one is reporting the real public opinion?" The correct answer to that cry is, "Neither one." But the reasonableness of that reply is not apparent when poll results are presented as objective facts comparable to objective facts about events. When that style of reporting is followed, opinion polls are more likely to confuse than enrich public debate.

Reporting Sampling Error
and Question Wordings

Ironically, even though poll results are typically reported in a descriptive, factual manner, all too often facts that professional pollsters consider essential to a valid interpretation of those results are not included. One of the most common, and glaring, omissions is the wording of the questions. Not reporting question wordings reinforces the impression that the percentages that are reported represent in themselves some "thing" we call public opinion. Without exact question wordings, readers have little chance of understanding that those percentages only tell us how a particular question about one aspect of an issue was answered, not how the opinion was formed or why.

The news media have resisted reporting question wordings despite efforts by professionals to get them to do so. In 1969, both the American Association for Public Opinion Research (a professional organization) and the National Council on Public Polls (a trade association) included both question wordings and allowances for sampling error in their standards of information that should be routinely reported in poll releases. The printed releases of poll results issued by all major polls, and less well-known polls as well, adhere to these standards. But question wordings are much less likely to be reported in the published stories or on televised reports than are statements on sampling error. For example, it is standard practice for CBS newscasters to read a statement on what allowance should be made for sampling error, whereas question wordings are hardly ever given.

The acceptance of reporting error allowances as a desideratum of responsible journalism to the exclusion of other criteria is evident in the treatment of sampling error in *Newsroom Guide to Polls and Surveys*,[38] an exemplary effort to guide newsroom personnel to understand, analyze, and report polls. The text correctly criticized one poll story for imputing importance to percentage differences that were statistically insignificant. However, the text failed to criticize the absence of the question wording in the story even though elsewhere the points were made that question wording could have a great influence on poll results[39] and that the patterning of all questions must be considered when reporting results.[40]

It would be a backward step if the practice of reporting sampling error were to be discontinued. Getting news editors to realize that reporting sampling error does not impugn a poll but adds to the accuracy of the news story was a difficult task. However, reporting sampling error without question wordings can only add to the misperception that the reported percentages have meaning in themselves. The double standard of reporting sampling error but not question wordings is a reflection of the psychology of journalism, in which questions are asked to ascertain facts about an event but are not important in themselves. Sampling error, on the other hand, is now deemed important enough to report because journalists have learned that it tells us something about the accuracy of the reported facts. Until news editors come to appreciate that the meaning of poll results lies as much in the wording of the questions asked as in the percentages and their precision, the news media will be unable to do a satisfactory job in reporting opinion polls descriptively, let alone analytically.

Reporting exact question wordings will not suffice, however, unless attention is also called to their significance. Some pollsters have tried to do this by including a cautionary statement in the methodological descriptions they add to their news releases. The *Baltimore Sun*, for example, in 1986 used the following sentence, developed by Hollander, Cohen Associates (the organization then polling for it) along with its standard statement on sampling error: "There are also non-sampling causes of variability, such as question wording, question sequence or interviewer differences." Few pollsters highlight the importance of question wording so sharply. If they make any mention of the importance of question wording, it is usually in the context of "practical problems" in conducting polls that are sources of nonsampling error. For example:

The Gallup Poll: "In addition to sampling error, the reader should bear in mind that question wording and practical difficulties in conducting surveys can introduce error or bias into the findings of opinion polls."

The California Poll: "The (reader) (viewer) (listener) should also be aware that there are other possible sources of error for which precise estimates cannot be calculated. For example, different question wording and undetected flaws in the way sampling and interviewing procedures were carried out could have a significant effect on the findings. Good polling practices diminish the chances of such errors, but they can never be entirely ruled out. It is also possible, of course, that events occurring since the time the interviews were conducted could have changed the opinions reported here."

The Minnesota Poll: "Other forms of error or bias might be introduced by question wording and the practical difficulties of conducting any survey."

A subtle, but significant, difference between the *Sun*'s statement and those of the Gallup, California, and Minnesota Polls is that the former refers to the effect of question design on the "variability" of poll results while the latter refer to "error or bias." The *Sun*'s statement implies that when two differently worded questions produce different results, this does not necessarily mean that one of those questions is in error or biased; it might only mean that the two questions ask about different aspects of an issue.

The "practical difficulties" and "undetected flaws" in conducting a poll mentioned in the Gallup, California, and Minnesota Poll statements refer more to the layperson's idea of "mistakes" than to the fact that two questions can be worded differently without one of them being "right" and the other "wrong." The Gallup and California Poll statements consequently draw the reader's attention away from the importance of specific question wordings when interpreting poll results. Instead, they tend to reinforce the perception of variability among polls as the result of mistakes and the assumption that there is a single question wording that will reveal the "true" public opinion on an issue.

This reinforcement is especially likely to occur in statements about nonsampling error, such as the following, that make no reference at all to question wording as a source of nonsampling variability:

New York Times: "In addition to sampling error, the practical difficulties of conducting any survey of public opinion may introduce other sources of error into the poll."

Los Angeles Times: "These theoretical sampling errors do not take into account a small margin of additional error resulting from the various practical difficulties in taking any survey of public opinion."

Despite the commendable efforts being made by some within the news media to further a technical understanding of polls,[41] as yet there has been little comparable effort to instill an understanding of what polls measure. That understanding cannot be achieved without reporting question wordings.

Practical Problems of Journalism

There are some very practical journalistic considerations that also explain why the news media have largely fallen short of the goal of interpretation in their reporting of opinion polls. These considerations include (1) the dullness of statistics; (2) budgetary, space, and time restrictions; and (3) the need to be timely.

The dullness of statistics

For most people, statistics are dull and boring. A string of percentages representing how people answered a long series of questions, plus an analysis of how different segments of the population—for example, blacks versus whites, young versus old, rich versus poor, educated versus not so well educated, Democrats versus Republicans, conservatives versus liberals—differed in their opinions, makes for an informative, but dull, story. There is little that will lose a television or newspaper audience faster than a string of numbers. This is why the typical poll story contains little more than a few percentages that summarize the replies of all respondents to a few questions. Even when a poll has probed an issue in some depth, common practice is to report the results for only a few key questions. The typical result is a superficial rendering that reports the poll as if it were a plebiscite. Even when the reporter has access to a detailed analysis, the reader is seldom privy to the specifics of that analysis.

Budgetary, space, and time restrictions

The cost of conducting opinion polls and the competition for space and time in which to report them also militate against analytical reporting. The cost of conducting a single modest poll that asks a few questions about a half-dozen issues and that is based on a sample too small for anything more than some straightforward tabulations would pay the annual salary of a cub reporter. The syndicated polls, such as Gallup and Harris, whose poll reports are released through subscribing newspapers, try to cope with financial pressures by designing each poll they conduct to produce nine to twelve news releases, with each release reporting the results of only a few questions in about 750 words. Sometimes those results are analyzed by demographic characteristics, but to control costs only a few standard characteristics are used. Even with these cost-cutting practices, syndicated opinion polls are not particularly profitable, often being little more than loss leaders for commercial surveys.

In addition to the syndicated polls, there are those that are commissioned by individual newspapers and stations on an ad hoc basis. Although the budgets for these polls are modest, they represent major expenditures for their sponsors. Therefore, these individually commissioned polls tend to be infrequent, are often based on relatively small samples so the results cannot be analyzed in detail, and deal almost exclusively with major hard-news events such as elections or terrorist attacks. These polls are not designed to provide an analytical understanding of public opinion. Polls conducted for news magazines tend to share these characteristics.

Even the polls conducted by the networks and major newspapers are subject to severe budget and space restrictions. One indication of cost pressures is that most polls sponsored by national media are joint ventures: CBS News and the *New York Times* poll jointly, as do ABC News and the *Washington Post* and as did NBC News and the *Wall Street Journal* in the past. At the state level, consortia of noncompetitive newspapers are occasionally formed to conduct statewide polls. Other newspapers have assigned polling to departments whose primary responsibility is marketing research. Many use in-house telephone resources (whose primary task is to solicit for subscribers) for interviewing, with faculty from nearby academic institutions serving as consultants.

In addition to these kinds of costsharing, budgets are controlled by limiting the number of polls conducted in a year. Except in election years, the television network/newspaper joint ventures conduct about four to six a year. Limiting the length of each interview to about twenty minutes or less is another common practice. (A nonbudgetary reason for conducting short interviews is the concern that public cooperation would be diminished with longer interviews.)

Space restrictions in print and time restrictions on television are another significant constraint on what can be reported by the news media. This constraint is particularly severe on television, which can seldom provide more than about a minute on evening news to report poll results. In the 1960s, CBS and NBC experimented with special half and full hour shows devoted to reporting poll results in some detail. Those programs were discontinued because they failed to generate audience interest. Newspapers have more flexibility, but except in election years even the *New York Times, Washington Post,* or *Los Angeles Times* will seldom free more than two full columns for a poll story.

The need to be timely

Because hard news is by definition timely, the further removed an opinion poll is from specific events of the day, the less timely (newsworthy) is it deemed to be. For this reason, there is a considerable perceived risk in reporting polls as anything other than hard news. From the narrowest of journalistic perspectives, the safest way to report a poll is to treat it as an event that has just occurred rather than as a basis for analyzing public opinion. This helps explain why a typical poll story is a description of what happened when a representative sample of the public was interviewed, not an analysis of public opinion.

Nevertheless, interest in the results of certain questions has become so high that such poll results are timely regardless of when the poll was conducted. Presidential popularity ratings are illustrative of these questions. "In the alchemy of journalism, a change in the president's popularity rating is not merely a survey result, it is something that has happened to his political strength, and therefore is news."[42] A particularly interesting aspect of this phenomenon is that the concept of presidential popularity rating is in largest part an artifact of polling itself. The question was invented at the Gallup Poll, which pioneered the practice of tracking presidential ratings to chart fluctuations in a president's political strength as a way of creating interest in polls during nonelection years. One consequence of this is that polling is transformed from a method that measures a presumably preexisting public opinion into a procedure that defines what public opinion is.

The need of journalists to avoid dullness, adjust to budget and space constraints, and maximize timeliness leaves little room for the kind of analytic reporting of opinion polls that would enrich public debate. Special formats are needed for reporting polls that will solve both the technical and substantive problems we have discussed. Background news and investigative reporting are models for reporting polls that already exist in journalism and that are far more appropriate than the hard-news format.

THE BACKGROUND-NEWS MODEL

There is an established journalistic tradition of supplementing hard news with background reporting that provides a highly appropriate model for reporting opinion polls. Background reporting seeks out information that helps place the events covered by hard news in perspective. This is done through a fuller reporting of objective facts related to but not necessarily part of specific events covered by daily news reports. Timeliness is preserved by tying the story to events of the day. Although background reporting goes beyond the chronicling of daily events, it is still driven by a focus on events and the objective facts surrounding them. As such, it is distinct from editorializing and presumes to be objective in the same sense that hard-news reporting is objective.

The Value of Reporting Polls as Background

If polls were reported as background rather than hard news, reports would not have to be restricted to a factual recounting of poll results. Instead of sheer description, the doors would be opened for analysis as well. Space would not be so restrictive a consideration because editorial decisions would have been made to make space available for a background story, eliminating the need to compete with the day's hard news for space.

A few polls are reported in this manner. A *New York Times*/CBS News Poll conducted on the eve of Reagan's 1987 State of the Union address is an excellent example of what can be done.[43] Because the address was scheduled for the evening of January 27, interviewing was timed so that the results would be available for that morning's paper. The story, which had front-page positioning and which ran about fifty-four column inches, presented the poll results as background information about the political context of the address. The lead paragraph in the article by E. J. Dionne, Jr., contrasted with the typical hard-news format: "President Reagan, fighting to revive his Presidency with his sixth State of the Union Message tonight, will address a nation that is deeply skeptical that he can achieve his goals and doubtful that he is telling the truth about Iran and the Nicaragua rebels, the latest New York Times/CBS News Poll shows."[44] The story went on not only to report the poll results but to relate them to continuing controversy about issues dominating the news, such as aid to the Nicaraguan contras, the Iran-contra affair, farm aid, student loans, and a nuclear arms agreement with the Soviet Union.

A *Washington Post* story written by David S. Broder, Haynes Johnson, and Paul Taylor is an example of how polls can be worked into background news without being tied to a specific event.[45] This story, which ran more than seventy column inches, related national poll results showing growing public disillusionment and pessimism to interviews that were conducted by the writers in a number of "ticket-splitting" election precincts. The story was not hard news but an analysis of how the public's mood was changing and what were the political consequences of that change.

Nonpolitical news events can also provide a setting for public opinion polls. An interesting example is a report on a poll of public opinion toward immigration that the *New York Times* published as part of its coverage of the centennial celebration of the restored Statue of Liberty.[46] Taking the timely and relevant celebration as the context, the story reported current public receptivity to admitting the "huddled masses" of the 1980s as immigrants.

When space is a problem, the occasional practice of incorporating background into hard news can be adopted. Blending appropriate poll results into hard news can add depth in a timely way without using much additional space. For example, in a *New York Times* story on Robertson's campaigning in Iowa a month prior to that state's 1988 presidential caucuses, Steven V. Roberts related Robertson's tactics to recent poll results that revealed the strongly negative image he had to overcome.[47]

The Background-News Approach
and Postelection Debate

The use of poll results to analyze the meaning of George Bush's victory in the 1988 presidential election is an example of how polls as background news can meaningfully contribute to public debate. The usual postelection debate as to what kind of mandate the victor had received was intensified in 1988 for two reasons. First, the election returns were contradictory, with the Republican Bush winning the presidency by a decisive margin while the Democrats slightly increased their control of Congress. Second, many maintained that as a result of the negative campaign tactics employed that year, the important issues facing the nation had been ignored during the campaign (according to the Harris Poll, that opinion was shared by 73 percent of the public).[48] As a result, it was not clear what policy desires voters had in mind when casting their ballots. Predictably, Republicans and conservatives came up with different interpretations of the meaning of the election from those offered by Democrats and liberals. Those differences had more to do with partisan and ideological predispositions than with an objective analysis.

Public opinion polls interjected into the debate information on the public's views as to what the nation's priorities should be and on their self-avowed reasons for voting as they did. According to a Gallup Poll conducted just before the election,[49] there was substantial majority agreement, among both Bush and Dukakis supporters, that top priority should be given to reducing the federal budget deficit, proposing laws to protect the environment, and negotiating further arms reductions with the Soviet Union. There was also broad agreement among adherents of both candidates that top priority should *not* be given to restoring diplomatic relations with Iran, postponing Social Security cost-of-living increases as a way of reducing the national debt, or increasing tariffs on Japanese imports. On other issues, however, there were sharp differences of opinion, with Dukakis supporters far more likely to believe that top priority should be given to creating a national health insurance plan, making it easier for people to buy their first home, and providing care for the children of working parents (see Table 4.1).

Exit polls—interviews with voters as they left their voting places that asked whom they had voted for, why, and what their opinions were on the leading issues of the day—cast further light on what the voting public wanted from the incoming administration. Sponsored by ABC, CBS, and NBC in association with, respectively, the *Washington Post,* the *New York Times,* and the *Wall Street Journal,* the results of those exit polls were used on election night to analyze the returns as they came in. They were also featured in the following morning's newspaper analyses of the election. While different strategies were employed by each newspaper in assessing President-elect Bush's presumptive mandate, their assessments, although not identical, were for the most part congruent.

TABLE 4.1
Identifying the "Mandate" of the 1988 Presidential Election

"Regardless of who is elected in November, there are a number of important issues the next president will face. For each of the following issues, please tell me whether you think it is very important and should be a top priority for the next administration, it's important but not a top priority, or whether it should not be considered at all."

	Named as top priority		
	All Adults (%)	Bush Supporters (%)	Dukakis Supporters (%)
Reducing the Federal budget deficit	76	76	78
Proposing laws to increase protection of the environment	64	60	70
Negotiating further arms reductions with the Soviet Union	63	64	64
Proposing laws to create a national health insurance plan	44	28	60
Developing a program to make it easier for people to buy their first home	40	32	47
Proposing a program to provide care for children while their parents are at work	39	29	52
Increasing tariffs on Japanese imports	35	35	35
Delaying cost-of-living increases for one year in order to reduce the Federal budget deficit	24	24	23
Restoring diplomatic relations with Iran	17	17	19

Source: Gallup Poll news release, November 6, 1988.

The *Washington Post* published a front-page story based on the joint ABC News/*Washington Post* exit polls. Focusing largely, although not exclusively, on demographic voting patterns, the story led with the statement that Bush's victory was accompanied by "significant erosions in the Reagan coalition—the right-leaning alliance that Republicans have been counting on to produce a sustained realignment of presidential voting patterns in the United States."[50] Weaker support for Bush than Reagan had achieved among middle-income and younger voters, union members, and voters of Eastern European ancestry was reported as evidence of this erosion. With respect to issues, the *Post* reported that Bush did best among voters for whom international affairs and defense were primary concerns, whereas Dukakis's strength was among those for whom social issues were an important voting influence. The death penalty, the Pledge of Allegiance, and prison furloughs were decisive issues for a minority of voters, but they voted overwhelmingly for Bush.

The *New York Times,* which integrated its exit poll results into its front-page lead story on the election, concluded that the exit polls it conducted with CBS News showed that "Mr. Reagan's popularity and the generally favorable assessments voters made of the nation's economy were key factors in Mr. Bush's victory. In addition, the poll also showed that Mr. Bush's own campaign clearly got through its central argument: that Mr. Bush was more experienced than Mr. Dukakis, better equipped to deal with military affairs and the Soviet Union, tougher on crime, and more likely to keep taxes down."[51] The *Times* story went on to note that not only was Dukakis strong among lower-income voters but that he "won back a substantial share of the Democrats who backed President Reagan in 1984."[52]

The *Wall Street Journal* published a feature story, headlined "Polls Show No Clear Consensus Among Voters About Direction New President Should Take," based on the exit polls conducted by NBC News. Asserting that "Americans voted yesterday for a man—but not a message,"[53] the *Wall Street Journal* reported that their polls found that (1) voters did not have a clear idea about what either candidate would do if elected president and (2) there was no clear consensus about the desired direction that the incoming president should take. Nonetheless, the polls did depict some significant trends. Half of those interviewed thought that reducing the federal budget deficit should be a top priority, although there was no agreement as to how that should be achieved. Furthermore, "large majorities agreed that the next president should seek further arms reductions with the Soviet Union and should do more to protect the environment and to ensure that all Americans have adequate health care—even if that would result in higher taxes."[54] The most frequent reasons cited for voting for Bush were "his competence and experience, his stand on defense issues, and his position on the economy and taxes. For Mr. Dukakis, the overwhelming attraction was his stand on domestic issues such as education and health."[55]

Regardless of how adequate or correct the foregoing poll stories may be, they contrasted in form and purpose with hard-news reports on how public opinion split on some proposed legislation or policy. Instead, they analyzed in some detail responses to a variety of questions in order to interpret public opinion. In this way, they provided background to the political event of the day, the presidential election, that became part of subsequent debate about Bush's mandate.

Without question, and as critics of polls would be quick to point out, these poll results did not define a thought-out domestic or foreign policy or a legislative program. But they did identify major trends in public thinking that provided considerable substance for public debate as a new administration entered office, a substance that went far beyond the partisan assertions that typified much political commentary on the election's "meaning." Unfortunately, the intensive and featured use of polls to provide background to the election results, as exemplified in these reports of exit poll results, is rare and is largely restricted to elections.

THE INVESTIGATIVE-REPORTING MODEL

Investigative reporting moves away from hard news by examining presumably important conditions even if a newsworthy event related to those conditions has not occurred. Acting as eyewitness and/or interviewer, the investigative reporter actively makes news by intervening in public affairs.[56] We must not forget that the intrusion of personal and organizational values and interests in the selection of what to report, never absent from hard-news reporting, can be a significant source of bias in investigative reporting.[57] Nonetheless, the appropriateness of this model for reporting poll results to provide insight regarding public opinion is evident in Bogart's comment: "A great bulwark of democracy is the tradition of investigative reporting in journalism, which stems from the initiative of the news-gathering organization. The essence of this kind of reporting is that it is done in depth, that it digs below the surface of events, that it deals with them not as incidents but as evidences of a deeper and more significant pattern."[58] By adopting the model of investigative reporting, public opinion polls on persistent but seemingly remote and abstract national problems can help make those problems of immediate interest without waiting for them to reach crisis proportions. As Bogart pointed out, "As soon as polls start to ask people's opinions about something, that subject becomes a matter of public debate."[59]

Precision Journalism

In the 1970s, Philip Meyer, a news reporter who became a polling specialist, developed the concept *precision journalism* to describe the application of polling to investigative and background reporting.[60] Since then, some major newspapers have taken steps in the direction of using investigative reporting as a model for the polls they conduct. Illustrative is the occasional practice of the *Los Angeles Times* of devoting an entire poll to an in-depth investigation of opinion on major issues such as poverty (April 1985), women at work and in politics (August 1984), and the death penalty (June 1985).

Two *New York Times* polls on race relations in New York City built upon the December 1986 Howard Beach incident (in which a gang of white teenagers attacked three black men) and the controversy surrounding the charges made by Tawana Brawley, a black teenager, that she had been raped by a gang of white men to investigate race attitudes.[61] Those polls used questions from an earlier poll on racial attitudes to investigate the public's beliefs regarding the trend in race relations in New York City and the fairness with which blacks were treated. These polls went beyond providing background to the Howard Beach and Brawley cases by investigating the conflicting attitudes that gave rise to those events.

A *New York Times* feature story on homelessness written by Michael Oreskes and Robin Toner incorporated poll results into an analysis of the sources of that problem and the difficulties policymakers were facing in dealing with it.[62] Public perceptions of the reasons leading to homelessness were measured by a series of questions on how much blame should be put on five possible factors: the domestic policies of the Reagan administration—24 percent: a lot [of blame]; local governments for failing to take care of people in need—30 percent: a lot; homeless people being unwilling to work—37 percent: a lot; mental institutions for releasing patients who are not able to lead normal lives—44 percent: a lot; and alcohol and drug abuse by the homeless—50 percent: a lot. Regardless of how accurate or inaccurate those perceptions may be, they are significant in that they define the public's understanding of the roots of homelessness and therefore the public's receptivity to proposed solutions.

FORMATS FOR REPORTING POLLS

Despite the occasional use of polls for background and investigative reporting, few newspapers ever apply these models for public opinion polling. The bulk of newspaper coverage of polls continues to adhere to the hard-news format. Television coverage uses almost no polls for background or investigative reporting. After failing in the 1960s to build background and investigative television shows around polls, television networks and channels now report polls almost exclusively as hard news. The use of polls by news magazines is equally restricted. Whereas in the 1960s *Newsweek* devoted major segments of an issue to a poll on a single topic, such as race relations or "middle America," today it typically does no more than report a few percentages in tabular form without even a reference to the table in the adjacent text. *Time* and *U.S. News and World Report* follow similar formats.

Even when background reporting and investigative reporting are adopted as models, reporting poll results in an informative and interesting manner remains a difficult problem. The core of this problem is how to combine analytic commentary with factual documentation and not lose the audience. On one hand, the mass of statistics needed to document a full analysis is far too much for a typical newspaper or magazine reader to pore through or for a television viewer to sit through. On the other hand, if the analysis were presented without the backup data, not only would the story's credibility be impaired but so would its informational value.

Currently, this dilemma is handled, although not solved, by both print and broadcast media in somewhat similar ways. In print media, a few generalized conclusions are reported, documented by a limited number of percentages in the text, perhaps supplemented by a few charts and tables summarizing the key results. On television, a few generalized conclusions are read, backed up by one or two simple graphics to provide visual interest. In both instances, to anyone who has had the opportunity to go through the complete tabulations that were available, the final story is a frustratingly incomplete picture of the richness of the data. Although this kind of reporting may be satisfactory for the cursory newspaper reader or viewer of televised evening news, it is clearly inadequate for political leaders and activists interested in learning about and understanding public opinion on issues of the day.

To compensate for the limited information available from the typical news reports on polls, some polls (such as CBS/*New York Times,* ABC/ *Washington Post,* and the *Los Angeles Times*) distribute tabulations of poll results and written commentary to selected mailing lists. These sources, however, do not satisfy the seemingly insatiable appetite of the politically active for poll data. This has created a market for publications that report polls in greater detail or scope than is available from the mass news media. The Gallup Poll has a monthly publication, *The Gallup Report,* available by subscription, that provides the results of all the questions asked on its regular polls, tabulated by a full set of standard demographic characteristics. A major feature of *Public Opinion* magazine is an analytical compilation of poll results on selected topics that change from issue to issue. The publishers of the *National Journal* sponsor a newsletter, *Opinion Outlook,* to bring together in a convenient form the results of available private polls as well as media-sponsored polls. *World Opinion Update* provides a bimonthly summary of polls on issues of international importance. During the 1988 campaign season, American Political Network offered a subscription service that, among others things, provided weekly analyses of political trends and events by well-known pollsters Patrick Caddell, Bill Hamilton, Peter Hart, Paul Maslin, Lance Tarrance, Robert Teeter, and Richard Wirthlin. Informative as these sources may be, they are accessible only to limited audiences. The segment of the general public that is politically involved and active—a segment that is of paramount political significance—has little opportunity to become aware of, let alone have access to, these sources.

Separating Statistics from Analysis

Guidance for developing a more satisfactory format that the general news media can use for reporting poll results to the politically alert general public comes from poll reports that are prepared for private clients. As to be expected, those reports contain analytical summaries of the meaning of the poll results, with a limited number of key percentages. In addition, at least as prepared by responsible pollsters, the reports also include appendices comprised of tables showing the detailed computer tabulations that back up the analytic text. The text focuses on the meaning of the results, but the backup data are always there for those who want to examine them and check the conclusions presented in the text. This format is efficient because the text does not have to carry the burden of what can be communicated most compactly in tabular form, and the meaning of the data is not overwhelmed by statistical detail. I suggest that the principle of separating statistical documentation from interpretive analysis when reporting poll results can be applied to both newspapers and television, although the technical characteristics of each medium require very different approaches to implementing the principle.

Print formats

Newspapers might consider separating stories from detailed statistics, which is the standard practice of their sports and financial sections. In a style analogous to that used for reporting box scores, league standings, and individual athletes' performance records or for reporting stock and bond prices, the tabulations of poll results could be printed in compact tables with priority given to clarity and conciseness rather than esthetics. The write-up on the poll could then concentrate on analyzing and interpreting the results in a style geared to the general newspaper reader and unencumbered by the need to provide a detailed statistical documentation within the story itself.

Some limited progress has been made by the *New York Times* in using this format for presenting its analyses of exit polls. As shown in Table 4.2, the *Times* has constructed a table shell that enables it to report the voting behavior of the U.S. electorate analyzed by detailed demographic characteristics. The director of the *Times* poll, Michael Kagay, has described this as a "supertable" that allows readers to interpret the results for themselves.[63] Irwin A. Lewis, director of the

TABLE 4.2
The New York Times/CBS NEWS Poll: Portrait of the Electorate

% of 1988 total		VOTE IN 1980			VOTE IN 1984		VOTE IN 1988	
		Reagan	Carter	Anderson	Reagan	Mondale	Bush	Dukakis
—	TOTAL	51%	41%	7%	59%	40%	53%	45%
48	Men	55	36	7	62	37	57	41
52	Women	47	45	7	56	44	50	49
85	Whites	55	36	7	64	35	59	40
10	Blacks	11	85	3	9	89	12	86
3	Hispanics	35	56	8	37	61	30	69
69	Married	—	—	—	62	38	57	42
31	Not married	—	—	—	52	46	46	53
20	18–29 years old	43	44	11	59	40	52	47
35	30–44 years old	54	36	8	57	42	54	45
22	45–59 years old	55	39	5	59	39	57	42
22	60 and older	54	41	4	60	39	50	49
8	Not a high school graduate	46	51	2	49	50	43	56
27	High school graduate	51	43	4	60	39	50	49
30	Some college education	55	35	8	61	37	57	42
35	College graduate or more	52	35	11	58	41	56	43
19	College graduate	—	—	—	—	—	62	37
16	Post graduate education	—	—	—	—	—	50	48
48	White Protestant	63	31	6	72	27	66	33
28	Catholic	49	42	7	54	45	52	47
4	Jewish	39	45	15	31	67	35	64
9	White fundamentalist or evangelical Christian	63	33	3	78	22	81	18
25	Union household	43	48	6	46	53	42	57
12	Family income under $12,500	42	51	6	45	54	37	62
20	$12,500–$24,999	44	46	7	57	42	49	50
20	$25,000–$34,999	52	39	7	59	40	56	44
20	$35,000–$49,999	59	32	8	66	33	56	42
24	$50,000 and over	63	26	9	69	30	62	37
19	$50,000–$100,000	—	—	—	—	—	61	38
5	Over $100,000	—	—	—	—	—	65	32
25	From the East	47	42	9	52	47	50	49
28	From the Midwest	51	40	7	58	40	52	47
28	From the South	52	44	3	64	36	58	41
19	From the West	53	34	10	61	38	52	46
35	Republicans	86	8	4	93	6	91	8
37	Democrats	26	67	6	24	75	17	82
26	Independents	55	30	12	63	35	55	43
18	Liberals	25	60	11	28	70	18	81
45	Moderates	48	42	8	53	47	49	50
33	Conservatives	72	23	4	82	17	80	19

TABLE 4.2 (Continued)

% of 1988 total		VOTE IN 1980			VOTE IN 1984		VOTE IN 1988	
		Reagan	Carter	Anderson	Reagan	Mondale	Bush	Dukakis
—	TOTAL	51%	41%	7%	59%	40%	53%	45%
31	Professional or manager	57	32	9	62	37	59	40
11	White-collar worker	50	41	8	59	40	57	42
13	Blue-collar worker	47	46	5	54	45	49	50
4	Full-time student	—	—	—	52	47	44	54
5	Teacher	46	42	10	51	48	47	51
5	Unemployed	39	51	8	32	67	37	62
10	Homemaker	—	—	—	61	38	58	41
2	Agricultural worker	36	59	4	—	—	55	44
16	Retired	—	—	—	60	40	50	49
56	1984 Reagan voters	75	9	2	100	0	80	19
9	1984 Democratic Reagan voters	57	23	2	100	0	48	51
28	1984 Mondale voters	14	63	8	0	100	7	92
23	Democratic primary voters	—	—	—	—	—	21	78
18	Republican primary voters	—	—	—	—	—	87	11
7	First time voters	—	—	—	61	38	51	47
41	White men	59	32	7	67	32	63	36
44	White women	52	39	8	62	—	56	43
5	Black men	14	82	3	12	84	15	81
5	Black women	9	88	3	7	93	9	90
10	Men, 18–29 years old	47	39	11	63	36	55	43
11	Women, 18–29 years old	39	49	10	55	44	49	50
17	Men, 30–44 years old	59	31	8	61	38	58	40
19	Women, 30–44 years old	50	41	8	54	45	50	49
11	Men, 45–59 years old	60	34	5	62	36	62	36
12	Women, 45–59 years old	50	44	5	57	42	52	48
11	Men, 60 and older	56	40	3	62	37	53	46
11	Women, 60 and older	52	43	4	58	42	48	52
16	Whites, 18–29 years old	48	38	12	68	31	60	39
3	Blacks, 18–29 year old	7	89	3	6	94	12	86
30	Whites, 30–44 years old	59	31	8	63	36	60	39
4	Blacks, 30–44 years old	12	84	3	10	89	13	85
19	Whites, 45–59 years old	59	34	5	65	34	63	36
2	Blacks, 45–59 years old	13	84	3	10	86	10	86
20	Whites, 60 and older	56	39	4	63	37	54	45
2	Blacks, 60 and older	20	77	3	15	81	9	90
34	Married men	—	—	—	64	35	60	39
35	Married women	—	—	—	59	41	54	46
14	Unmarried men	—	—	—	55	42	51	47
17	Unmarried women	—	—	—	49	50	42	57
18	Republican men	87	8	4	94	5	91	8
17	Republican women	85	10	5	93	7	90	9
16	Democratic men	29	63	6	27	72	18	80

(Continues)

TABLE 4.2 (Continued)
The New York Times/CBS NEWS Poll: Portrait of the Electorate

% of 1988 total		VOTE IN 1980			VOTE IN 1984		VOTE IN 1988	
		Reagan	Carter	Anderson	Reagan	Mondale	Bush	Dukakis
21	Democratic women	23	71	5	21	78	16	84
13	Independent men	60	27	10	66	32	58	49
13	Independent women	49	34	13	59	39	52	46
27	White Democrats	30	62	6	29	70	21	79
7	Black Democrats	4	94	2	3	96	4	95
4	Men with less than high school education	51	47	2	52	47	49	50
4	Women with less than high school education	41	55	2	46	52	38	62
12	Male high school graduates	53	42	3	62	37	50	49
15	Female high school graduates	50	44	5	58	41	50	50
13	Men with some college	59	31	8	65	33	60	38
17	Women with some college	52	39	8	58	41	54	45
19	Male college graduates	58	28	11	63	36	63	36
16	Female college graduates	42	44	12	52	47	49	51
21	Whites in the East	51	38	10	57	42	54	45
2	Blacks in the East	12	85	3	7	90	12	85
25	Whites in the Midwest	55	37	7	64	35	57	42
2	Blacks in the Midwest	11	84	4	6	92	8	91
23	Whites in the South	61	35	3	71	28	67	32
4	Blacks in the South	9	89	2	10	89	12	86
15	Whites in the West	55	32	10	66	33	58	41
2	Blacks in the West	Insufficient data available					13	83

1988 data based on questionnaires completed by 11,645 voters leaving polling places around the nation on Election Day. 1984 data based on questionnaires from 9,174 voters; 1980 data based on questionnaires from 15,201 voters. Those who gave no answer are not shown. Dashes indicate that a question was not asked in a particular year.

Family income categories in 1980: Under $10,000, $10,000–14,999, $15,000–24,999, $25,000–49,999, and $50,000 and over. "Fundamentalist or evangelical Christian" was labeled "born-again Christian" in 1980 and 1984. Male and female college graduates include post graduate education.

How the Poll Was Taken

The New York Times/CBS News exit poll is based on questionnaires completed by voters as they left polling places throughout the United States on Tuesday [November 8, 1988]. The poll included 11,645 voters in 293 randomly selected precincts.

In theory, in 19 cases out of 20, the results based on such samples should differ by no more than one percentage point in either direction from what would have been obtained by seeking out all voters in the United States.

The potential sampling error for smaller subgroups is larger. For example, for black voters it is plus or minus three percentage points, and for Jewish voters it is plus or minus six percentage points.

In addition to sampling error, the practical difficulties of conducting any survey of voter opinion on Election Day may introduce other sources of error into the poll.

Los Angeles Times poll, has called for more interpretive reporting of poll results in place of simple recitation of numbers.[64]

The interest of general readers for news stories that add to their knowledge of the political scene without drowning them in an ocean of statistics would be satisfied by this approach, as would the need of political analysts and other inveterate poll watchers for detailed data. By adopting this approach, or others designed to achieve the same end, newspapers could analyze poll results in a way that highlights their significance to public debate on current issues.

Visual formats

Television obviously requires a different approach. Shows such as "Meet the Press," "Face the Nation," and the "McNeil-Lehrer News Hour" suggest the type of setting that might work and the kind of audience that could be attracted. Panelists would be provided, in advance of the show, with a written report containing an analytical summary of poll findings plus detailed tabulations—similar to the type of reports private pollsters provide their clients. The program would focus on how the panelists evaluate the meaning and significance of the poll results, not on the hopeless task of presenting those statistics on television in an interesting manner. A major task of the moderator would be to keep referring panelists to the poll findings when presenting their ideas and interpretations. This would serve to familiarize the audience with much of the poll's findings in an interesting and chal-lenging way. The feasibility of inviting interested viewers to buy copies of the written report might also be investigated. Public debate on the issue covered by the poll would be stimulated by telecasting this kind of exchange of ideas generated by the poll's findings instead of the boring statistics.

The thrust of both the preceding suggestions is to give salience to the meaning of poll results without ignoring the data. Some such approach is necessary if the news media are to serve as an effective channel for introducing opinion poll data into public debate in a responsible manner. The specifics of each suggestion are less significant than the intent. Other approaches may prove to be more practical and/or effective. But unless the news media adopt innovative methods for reporting polls, in preference to the staleness of what is now the common practice, the likelihood is that public opinion polls will continue to contribute far more to the manipulative repertoire of politicians than to their responsible responsiveness to the public.

CONCLUSION

The robustness of democracy in the United States depends on far more than public opinion polls. Nonetheless, a creative use of polling that conforms to what is methodologically valid can make a positive contribution to our democratic way of life. By giving policymakers a better understanding of the public's thinking and making them more sensitive to the public's needs and aspirations, public opinion polls can contribute to a more effective democracy. Walter Lippmann is often cited as saying that direct rule by public opinion results in either failure or tyranny. Even if we accept the validity of that observation, it is also true that ignoring public opinion does the same. Instead of opposing responsiveness to responsibility, effective democratic government depends on joining the two. Public opinion polls, if properly understood and utilized, can play a role in furthering that end.

Democracy exists in an ongoing process of public debate about what government should do and how. The most important contribution that polls can make to that process is to introduce the wants and needs of all sectors of the public into that debate as fully and accurately as possible. For this, polls are needed that analyze public opinion, with the results of those analyses objectively reported to the public. Although the news media provide what is probably the most suitable setting for such polls, to date few media-sponsored polls measure up to what is needed. Whether the potential of public opinion polls for strengthening democratic government will ever be realized depends largely on the readiness of the news media to make *full* use of what polls can tell us about public opinion. Failing that, media polls are likely to remain little more than news gimmicks, quasiplebiscites that provide a simplistic, confusing, and distorted understanding of public opinion. At the same time, privately commissioned polls would then continue to add to the ability of politicians and special interests to manipulate the public—without any effective countervailing force.

The news media themselves do not constitute a completely neutral political force and in fact are part of the concentration of power in contemporary society. Yet they also represent one of the few institutional settings in the United States that has the resources to sponsor polls, the means to inform the total public as to the results of those polls, and a professional ideology that values objectivity and public service. If they do not assume the responsibility of conducting and reporting polls in an incisive manner, it is unlikely that anyone else will do so.

 **5**

POLLS IN THE SERVICE
OF DEMOCRACY

Public opinion develops and makes itself felt through communications among members of the general public, special interest groups, and political leaders. Its building blocks are the opinions of individuals, but those opinions develop and derive their significance and force through communications. These communications occur in relation to specific situations in which personal and group interests and/or values are felt to be at stake. Thus understood, public opinion is a social process in constant flux, always changing in focus, direction, and definitiveness in reaction to both direct personal experiences and to the appeals of those who have control or access to mass communications.

To the extent that the linkage between public opinion and government is weakened, political unrest may arise. Democratic societies seek to maintain the linkage between public opinion and government through periodic elections. But given the dynamic nature of public opinion, elections can never be more than partial, transitory expressions of public opinion. Moreover, public opinion exists in the interstices of an organized polity. It comes to the fore when customary, institutionalized ways of deciding policy do not suffice. In the normal course of events, democracies rely on deliberative actions by their elected legislatures and executive leaders to set and implement public policies. As conditions of life change and new needs and problems arise, those deliberations may need new input from the public. It is then that public opinion can become a significant political force, if it is able to express itself.

Polls of public opinion provide a means for tracing the continuous movement of public opinion. In this way, they can help fill in the gap between the results of past elections and changing public opinion. Imperfect as they often are, polls are a way of learning things about the nature of public opinion that would otherwise be unknown. They can get at facets of public opinion that would otherwise be unexpressed and would therefore remain powerless as a political force. Properly used, polls can contribute to the maintenance of a strong linkage between the governed and those who govern them that is responsive and responsible to the needs and wants of the body politic.

The early pollsters assumed that polls would inevitably help strengthen democratic political processes. For a number of reasons, however, that assumption has proved to be naive. As we have seen, one of the major pitfalls in the use of public opinion polls is the habit of treating public opinion as measured by polls as a static object or event comparable to elections. But public opinion is a dynamic social process that, on occasion, mobilizes and is expressed in some form of collective action—voting and rioting in the streets are polar examples of such action. We have also seen that public opinion polls cannot serve as unqualified expressions of a "general will" of the people that exists even when not mobilized. Instead, at their best polls can serve as soundings of various aspects of a complex and continuously changing public psychology. For this reason, using polls as plebiscites, as mandates that political leaders are obligated to follow, is not only philosophically but methodologically fallible; public opinion cannot be encompassed in a single or even a few percentages.

Some critics of polls have argued that by bypassing group leaders, polls weaken the ability of the public to organize in politically effective ways.[1] There is no question that when polls reveal discongruities between formal group leaders and rank-and-file-members, they undermine the ability of those leaders to act as spokespersons for their constituencies. But it does not serve democracy if interest group leaders speak for their own purposes and not for their constituencies. In fact, as documented by uncounted polls, the 1970s and 1980s were marked by a decline in public confidence in all major institutions that reflected an alienation from "bigness" in all its manifestations—Big Government, Big Business, and Big Labor alike. The problem is not so much that formal leaders have been bypassed but that they have lost the confidence of their constituencies. One path to regaining that confidence is through polls that give leaders a fresh appreciation of what are the real priorities and aspirations of their presumed followers.

Of greatest concern in our analysis is the fact that polls can as easily serve manipulative as democratic purposes. To date, the role of public opinion polls has been primarily instrumental—that is, in their usefulness for developing election campaigns and other efforts to manipulate the public. Although some of the nation's leaders may have become more responsive to the public as a result of this application, it is also the case that their manipulative control of the public has been enhanced by this use of polls. If polls are used only, or pre-dominantly, to increase the manipulative efficacy of the politically powerful, they can have only a corrosive effect on democracy. For polls to strengthen democracy, they must function in the service of the community at large and not become the exclusive property of entrenched interest groups.

The ultimate goal of our analysis has been to consider the practices and institutional settings that would lead to a positive role for polls in a democracy. There is a pressing need for a medium through which ordinary citizens can voice their opinions, clearly and without distortion. Although media-sponsored polls have not as yet served this need well, they do have a potential for doing so. But that potential will not be realized until and unless the news media conduct polls that are based on a valid understanding of the nature of public opinion and then report them in a way that enhances rather than displaces public debate. In the absence of such a development, the continued and expanded use of polls is more likely to undermine than strengthen democracy. If the news media fulfill the potential as we have described it, polls will strengthen democracy by stimulating rather than replacing public debate.

NOTES

CHAPTER 1: POLLS AND PUBLIC OPINION

1. Claude E. Robinson, *Straw Votes* (New York: Columbia University Press, 1932).

2. George Gallup and Saul Rae, *The Pulse of Democracy* (New York: Simon and Schuster, 1940).

3. Lindsay Rogers, *The Pollsters* (New York: Knopf, 1949).

4. Gallup and Rae, *The Pulse of Democracy*, p. 12.

5. Ibid., p. 11.

6. Quoted in John M. Fenton, *In Your Opinion* (Boston: Little, Brown, 1960), p. x.

7. Rogers, *The Pollsters*, p. 213.

8. Walter Lippmann, *The Public Philosophy* (Boston: Little, Brown, 1955), pp. 32–33.

9. Ibid., p. 30.

10. Ibid., pp. 29–30.

11. Ibid., p. 185.

12. Gallup and Rae, *The Pulse of Democracy*, p. 46.

13. Ibid., p. 8.

14. Rogers, *The Pollsters*, pp. 10–11.

15. Herbert Blumer, "Public Opinion and Public Opinion Polling," *American Sociological Review* 13, no. 5 (1948): Rejoinder to Woodward and Newcombe, p. 554.

16. Ibid., p. 543.

17. Julian Woodward, "Discussion of Blumer," *American Sociological Review* 13, no. 5 (1948):552–554.

18. Theodore M. Newcombe, "Discussion of Blumer," *American Sociological Review,* 13, no. 5 (1948):549–552.

19. Robert Erickson and Norman Luttbeg, *American Public Opinion: Its Origins, Content and Impact* (New York: Wiley, 1973), p. 23.

20. Leo Bogart, *Silent Politics* (New York: Wiley-Interscience, 1972), p. 15.

21. Gallup and Rae, *The Pulse of Democracy,* p. 13.

22. Ibid., p. 8.

23. Jerome S. Bruner, *Mandate from the People* (New York: Duell, Sloan, and Pearce, 1944), p. 3.

24. Ibid., pp. 4–5. A contrasting view is that polls weaken the effective expression of public opinion precisely because they bypass organizational leaders and go directly to the rank and file. Ginsberg, for example, maintained that this reduces the effectiveness of those leaders in representing the needs and interests of their constituencies. See Benjamin Ginsberg, *The Captive Public: How Mass Opinion Promotes State Power* (New York: Basic Books, 1986), pp. 73–75.

25. Gallup and Rae, *The Pulse of Democracy,* p. 18. The difficulties inherent in analyzing election returns to determine public opinion have been emphasized by political scientists. V. O. Key, for example, in analyzing the maintenance of the New Deal coalition first established in the 1930s, observed, "One must go beyond the broad electoral verdict and examine the detailed movements in voter sentiment underlying the grand totals." V. O. Key, Jr., *The Responsible Electorate* (Cambridge, Mass.: Belknap Press, 1966), p. 33.

26. Gallup and Rae, ibid., p. 6.

27. Ibid., pp. 13–14.

28. Ibid., p. 15.

29. Elisabeth Noelle-Neumann, *The Spiral of Science* (Chicago: University of Chicago Press, 1984), p. 170.

30. M. Margolis, "Public Opinion as a Dependent Variable" (paper presented at the Annual Meeting of the American Political Science Association, New Orleans, Louisiana, 1985).

31. Gallup and Rae, *The Pulse of Democracy,* p. 9.

32. Ibid., pp. 4–6.

33. John F. O'Sullivan, "Finally, Acknowledging the Mandate," *New York Times,* November 11, 1988, p. A31.

34. Harold Mendelsohn and Irving Crespi, *Polls, Television and the New Politics* (Scranton, Penn.: Chandler Publishing, 1970), p. 26.

35. Leonard Doob, *Public Opinion and Propaganda* (New York: Henry Holt, 1948), p. 159.

36. Ibid., p. 161.

37. Ibid., pp. 162–164.

38. Norman R. Luttbeg, *Public Opinion and Public Policy* (Homewood, Ill.: Dorsey Press, 1974), p. 3.

39. Ibid., pp. 4–5.

CHAPTER 2: HOW POLLS ARE USED

1. Conversations with Paul Perry, president of the Gallup Organization from 1956 to 1980 (retired).

2. Conversations during 1980 with Burns Roper, President, The Roper Organization.

3. Frederick Mosteller, Herbert Hyman, Philip J. McCarthy, Eli S. Marks, and David B. Truman, *The Pre-election Polls of 1948* (New York: Social Science Research Council, 1948), p. vii.

4. Andy Logan, "Around City Hall," *New Yorker,* August 29, 1988, p. 77.

5. Irving Crespi, "The Case of Presidential Popularity," in A. Cantril, ed., *Polling on the Issues* (Cabin John, Md.: Seven Locks Press, 1980).

6. *New York Times,* January 25, 1987, p. 18.

7. Adam Clymer, *New York Times,* May 11, 1986, p. 22.

8. Harold Mendelsohn and Irving Crespi, *Polls, Television and the New Politics* (Scranton, Penn.: Chandler Publishing, 1970), pp. 16–17.

9. Sidney Blumenthal, "Marketing the President," *New York Times Magazine,* September 3, 1981, p. 43.

10. See *The Gallup Report* (July 1988):19.

11. *New York Times,* February 23, 1988, p. D28.

12. *The Political Resources Directory* (Rye, N.Y.: Carol Hess Associates, 1988).

13. The 1964 estimate is from Dan Nimmo, *The Political Persuaders* (Englewood Cliffs, N.J.: Prentice-Hall, 1970), p. 87. The 1984 estimate is from conversation with Leo Bogart, Executive Vice-President, Newspaper Advertising Bureau, May 1988.

14. Nimmo, ibid., p. 87.

15. Keith Haller, a private pollster, reported that the cost of one telephone interview for a standard opinion poll had risen from $25 in 1984 to $34 in 1988. *New York Times,* February 6, 1988, p. 9.

16. See Nimmo, *The Political Persuaders,* pp. 89–94, for a description of the initial stages of this replacement.

17. Elizabeth Drew, "Letter from Washington," *New Yorker,* April 4, 1988, pp. 75–91.

18. Irving Crespi, *Pre-election Polling: Sources of Accuracy and Error* (New York: Russell Sage Foundation, 1988), p. 77.

19. *Public Opinion* (July-August 1988):35.

20. Charles W. Roll and Albert H. Cantril, *Polls: Their Use and Misuse in Politics* (New York: Basic Books, 1972), p. 55.

21. Peter Boyer, "The Yuppies of Mississippi," *New York Times Magazine,* February 18, 1988, p. 40.

22. Roll and Cantril, *Polls: Their Use and Misuse,* pp. 4–5.

23. Nathan Glazer and Daniel Patrick Moynihan, *Beyond the Melting Pot* (Cambridge, Mass.: MIT Press, 1963), pp. 305–309.

24. *Time,* May 31, 1968, p. 19.

25. "Week in Review," *New York Times,* February 28, 1988, p. E6.

26. *New York Times,* August 7, 1987, p. A18.

27. For further discussion of this issue, see Irving Crespi, "American Reaction to President Carter's Call for a Boycott of the Moscow Olympics" (paper presented at the American Association for Public Opinion Research Conference,

King's Island, Ohio, May 31, 1980); Crespi, "The Case of Presidential Popularity"; and Irving Crespi, "Polls as Journalism," *Public Opinion Quarterly* 44 (1980):462–477.

28. Irving Crespi, "Social Security and the Polls: No Ado About Something," *Public Opinion* (October-November 1982):19.

29. See Committee on Government Operations, Research and Technical Programs Subcommittee, *The Use of Social Research in Federal Domestic Programs* (Washington, D.C.: GPO, April 1967).

30. *New York Times,* February 4, 1988, p. B1.

31. *New York Times,* February 7, 1988, p. 29.

32. *Newark Star-Ledger,* March 2, 1988, p. A-1.

33. Ibid.

34. Ibid.

35. Bernard Roshco, "Preface," in John Robinson and Robert Meadow, *Polls Apart* (Cabin John, Md.: Seven Locks Press, 1982), p. xiii.

36. Hadley Cantril, *The Human Dimension: Experiences in Policy Research* (New Brunswick, N.J.: Rutgers University Press, 1967), p. 44.

37. Roshco, "Preface," p. xv.

38. Ibid.

39. James Fallows, "The User's Perspective: A Round Table on the Impact of the Polls," in Albert H. Cantril, ed., *Polling on the Issues* (Cabin John, Md.: Seven Locks Press, 1980), p. 134.

40. Ibid., p. 142.

41. Quoted in Roshco, "Preface," p. xv.

42. Cited in John Robinson and Robert Meadow, *Polls Apart* (Cabin John, Md.: Seven Locks Press, 1982), p. 21.

43. A. Cantril, *Polling on the Issues,* pp. 138–139.

44. ABC News/*Washington Post* Poll #0196.

45. Gallup Poll news release, February 13, 1986.

46. Gallup Poll news release, May 21, 1987.

47. ABC News/*Washington Post* Poll #0196.

48. CBS News/*New York Times* Poll news release, January 27, 1986.

49. CBS News/*New York Times* Poll news release, February 25, 1986.

50. Gallup Poll news release, February 16, 1986.

51. ABC News/*Washington Post* Poll #0196.

52. Gallup Poll news release, March 19, 1986.

53. CBS News/*New York Times* Poll news release, April 14, 1986.

54. ABC News/*Washington Post* Poll #0198.

55. *Los Angeles Times* Poll no. 100.

56. Gallup Poll news release, June 8, 1986.

57. Roll and Cantril, *Polls: Their Use and Misuse,* pp. 41–42.

58. *New York Times,* February 2, 1988, p. 58.

59. Ibid.

60. Leo Bogart, *Silent Politics* (New York: Wiley-Interscience, 1972), pp. 10–12.

61. Albert H. Cantril and Charles Roll, Jr., *Hopes and Fears of the American People* (New York: Universe Books, 1971).

62. Ibid., frontispiece.

63. Stanley Elam, *The Gallup Polls of Attitudes Toward Education, 1969–1973* (Bloomington, Ind.: Phi Delta Kappa, 1973).

64. *New York Times,* October 5, 1988, p. B13.

65. *New York Times,* November 29, 1987, p. 27.

66. Ibid.

67. Conversation with Michael Kagay, Director of News Surveys, *New York Times.*

68. Conversation with Neil Upmeyer, Vice-President, The Gallup Organization.

69. *New York Times,* September 27, 1988, p. A14.

70. Compare with Benjamin Ginsberg, *The Captive Public: How Mass Opinion Promotes State Power* (New York: Basic Books, 1986), pp. 68–69.

CHAPTER 3: THE METHODOLOGY AND MEANING OF POLLS

1. See, for example, Earl R. Babbie, *The Practice of Social Research* (Belmont, Calif.: Wadsworth, 1975); Don A. Dillman, *Mail and Telephone Surveys: The Total Design Method* (New York: Wiley, 1978); C. A. Moser and G. Kalton, *Survey Methods in Social Investigation* (New York: Basic Books, 1972); Norman N. Bradburn and Seymour Sudman and Associates, *Improving Interview Methods and Questionnaire Design* (San Francisco: Jossey-Bass, 1979); Stanley Payne, *The Art of Asking Questions* (Princeton, N.J.: Princeton University Press, 1951); Ronald Andersen, Judith Kasper, and Martin R. Frankel and Associates, *Total Survey Error* (San Francisco: Jossey-Bass, 1979); Leslie Kish, *Survey Sampling* (New York: Wiley, 1965); Seymour Sudman, *Applied Sampling* (New York: Academic Press, 1970); and Donald Warwick and Charles A. Lininger, *The Sample Survey: Theory and Practice* (New York: McGraw-Hill, 1975).

2. Herbert Asher, *Polling and the Public: What Every Citizen Should Know* (Washington, D.C.: Congressional Quarterly Press, 1988); and Norman N. Bradburn and Seymour Sudman, *Polls and Surveys: Understanding What They Tell Us* (San Francisco: Jossey-Bass, 1988).

3. Andersen et al., *Total Survey Error.*

4. Irving Crespi, *Pre-election Polling: Sources of Accuracy and Error* (New York: Russell Sage Foundation, 1988), pp. 23–25.

5. Ibid., p. 25.

6. Ibid., p. 69.

7. Ibid., pp. 68–73.

8. *Washington Post,* February 18, 1988.

9. Warren Mitofsky, "The 1980 Pre-election Polls: A Review of Disparate Methods and Results" (paper presented at the annual meeting of the American Statistical Association, Detroit, August 10–13, 1981).

10. Crespi, *Pre-election Polling,* p. 136.

11. *New York Times,* March 31, 1988, p. B8.

12. Ibid.

13. Ibid.

14. Ibid.

15. See, for example, Paul F. Lazarsfeld, Bernard Berelson, and Hazel Gaudet, *The People's Choice* (New York: Columbia University Press, 1948).

16. Conversations with Warren Mitofsky, Director, Election and Survey Unit, CBS News, and Andrew Kohut, President, The Gallup Organization.

17. *Washington Post,* November 9, 1988, p. 1.

18. Gallup Poll news release, November 8, 1988.

19. Communication from Andrew Kohut, President, The Gallup Organization.

20. CBS News/*New York Times* Poll news release, December 16, 1987.

21. Charles W. Roll and Albert H. Cantril, *Polls: Their Use and Misuse in Politics* (New York: Basic Books, 1972), p. 19.

22. Crespi, *Pre-election Polling,* p. 130.

23. Irving Crespi, "Structural Sources of the George Wallace Constituency," *Social Science Quarterly* (June 1971):115–132.

24. "Favorite in May Is Favorite in Fall, Too," *New York Times,* May 17, 1988, p. A22.

25. Henry F. Gaff, "Maybe Bush Has Already Won," *New York Times,* August 27, 1988, Op-Ed page.

26. Irving Crespi, "The Case of Presidential Popularity," in A. Cantril, ed., *Polling on the Issues* (Cabin John, Md.: Seven Locks Press, 1980), p. 35; and Burns Roper, "Presidential Popularity: Do People Like the Actor or His Actions?" *Public Opinion* 6, no. 5 (1983):42–44.

27. In Gary Orren, "Presidential Popularity Ratings: Another View," *Public Opinion* 1, no. 2 (1978):35.

28. William R. Dillon, Thomas J. Madden, and Neil H. Firtle, *Marketing Research in a Marketing Environment* (St. Louis: Times Mirror/Mosby College Publishing, 1987), p. 316.

29. Lee Sigelman and Stanley Presser, "Measuring Public Support for the New Christian Right: The Perils of Point Estimation," *Public Opinion Quarterly* 52 (1988):325–337.

30. John Simpson, "Moral Issues and Status Politics," in R. Liebman and R. Withnow, eds., *The New Christian Right* (New York: Aldine, 1983).

31. Sigelman and Presser, "Measuring Public Support," p. 330.

32. Crespi, "The Case of Presidential Popularity"; and Roper, "Presidential Popularity."

33. Irving Crespi and Dwight Morris, "Question Order Effects on Voting Preferences in 1982," *Public Opinion Quarterly* 48 (1984):578–591.

34. Ibid.

35. Ibid.

36. Richard Morin, "Behind the Numbers: Confessions of a Pollster," *Washington Post,* October 16, 1988, p. C1.

37. Conversation with Professor Philip Meyer, University of North Carolina, Chapel Hill.

38. Morin, "Behind the Numbers."

39. Roll and Cantril, *Polls: Their Use and Misuse.*

40. *The Gallup Report* (June 1986):20, 23.

41. Gladys Engel Lang and Kurt Lang, *The Battle for Public Opinion* (New York: Columbia University Press, 1983), p. 116.

42. Elisabeth Noelle-Neumann, *The Spiral of Silence* (Chicago: University of Chicago Press, 1984).

43. Louis Guttman, "The Basis for Scalogram Analysis," in S. A. Stouffer, L. Guttman, E. A. Suchman, P. F. Lazarsfeld, S. A. Star, and J. E. Clausen, *Measurement and Prediction* (Princeton, N.J.: Princeton University Press, 1950).

44. John H. Shapiro, Kelly P. Patterson, Judith Russell, and John T. Young, "The Polls: Public Assistance," *Public Opinion Quarterly* 51 (1987):120–130.

45. Louis Guttman and Edward A. Suchman, "Intensity and a Zero Point for Attitude Analysis," *American Sociological Review* 12, no. 1 (1947):57–67.

46. See *The Gallup Opinion Index* (April 1978):27–29; and *The Gallup Monthly Report* (July 1981):21–22.

47. Poll #176, *Los Angeles Times* (n.d., mimeo).

48. *The Gallup Opinion Index* (April 1978):27–29; *The Gallup Monthly Report* (July 1981):21–22.

49. John Robinson and Robert Meadow, *Polls Apart* (Cabin John, Md.: Seven Locks Press, 1982), pp. 42–45.

50. Ibid.

51. Gallup Poll news release, December 7, 1987.

52. *The Gallup Opinion Index* (June 1967):11.

53. Eagleton Institute news release, September 15, 1985.

54. Gallup Poll news release, September 18, 1988.

55. Lang and Lang, *The Battle for Public Opinion*, p. 116.

56. Crespi, *Pre-election Polling*, pp. 104–108.

57. Irving Crespi, "How 'Hard-Hat' Is the Public on Crime?" *Columbia Journalism Review* (September-October 1975):40–41.

58. Ibid.

59. Roll and Cantril, *Polls: Their Use and Misuse*, p. 114.

60. Hadley Cantril, *Gauging Public Opinion* (Princeton, N.J.: Princeton University Press, 1944).

61. *GSS News*, no. 2. (September 1988):2.

62. *The Gallup Opinion Index* (November 1967):2–3.

63. *The Gallup Report* (July 1988):18.

CHAPTER 4: POLLS, NEWS MEDIA, AND PUBLIC DEBATE

1. George Gallup, *The Sophisticated Poll Watchers Guide* (Princeton, N.J.: Princeton Opinion Press, 1972), pp. 3, 21.

2. Benjamin Ginsberg, *The Captive Public: How Mass Opinion Promotes State Power* (New York: Basic Books, 1986), p. 68.

3. Personal observation.

4. See, for example, *The Times* (Trenton), September 27, 1988, p. A1.

5. See, for example, "Round One Undecisive: Neither Candidate Is a Winner," *New York Times,* September 27, 1988, p. B6.

6. Gallup Poll news release, October 30, 1988.

7. *Los Angeles Times* mailing, July 20, 1986.

8. *New York Times,* August 7, 1988, p. 22.

9. Gallup Poll news release, October 16, 1988.

10. *New York Times,* 1988.

11. William D. Wells, "Psychographics: A Critical Review," *Journal of Marketing Research* 2 (1975):198.

12. Irving Crespi, "American Reaction to President Carter's Call for a Boycott of the Moscow Olympics" (paper presented at the American Association for Public Opinion Research Conference, King's Island, Ohio, May 31, 1980).

13. Leo Bogart, *Silent Politics* (New York: Wiley-Interscience, 1972), pp. 11-12.

14. Irving Crespi, "The Political Significance of Public Opinion Regarding the Need and Justification for U.S. Involvement in Vietnam" (paper presented at the American Sociological Association, New York, August 27, 1973).

15. Hadley Cantril, *Politics of Despair* (New York: Basic Books, 1958), Chap. 1.

16. *New York Times,* March 15, 1966, p. 1.

17. CBS News Poll news release, March 1982, part 4.

18. *The Gallup Report* (July 1981):21.

19. CBS News Poll news release, January 21, 1989.

20. Ibid., pp. 20, 22.

21. *The Gallup Opinion Index* (April 1978):27-29.

22. *The Times* (Trenton), April 9, 1989, p. A15.

23. E. J. Dionne, "Poll Finds Ambivalence on Abortion Persists in U.S.," *New York Times,* August 3, 1989, p. A18.

24. Ginsberg, *The Captive Public,* p. 65.

25. Irving Crespi, "The Pesky Preprimary Polls," *Public Opinion* (1988):48-50.

26. Conversation with Karlyn Keene, November 1988.

27. Bernard Roshco, *Newsmaking* (Chicago: University of Chicago Press, 1975), pp. 12-14.

28. Ibid.; and Doris A. Graber, *Mass Media and American Politics* (Washington, D.C.: Congressional Quarterly Press, 1980), pp. 63-65.

29. Irving Crespi, "Polls as Journalism," *Public Opinion Quarterly* 44 (1980):462-477.

30. *New York Times,* November 16, 1987.

31. *New York Times,* December 17, 1987.

32. *Washington Post,* June 3, 1987.

33. *Los Angeles Times,* May 10, 1987.

34. Gallup Poll news release, September 13, 1987.

35. Harris Survey news release, August 16, 1986.

36. *New York Times,* June 25, 1986.

37. Gallup Poll news release, July 13, 1986.

38. G. Cleveland Wilhoit and David H. Weaver, *Newsroom Guide to Polls and Surveys* (Washington, D.C.: American Newspaper Publishers Association, 1980).

39. Ibid., p. 56.

40. Ibid., p. 60.

41. Ibid.; Richard Morin, "Behind the Numbers: Confessions of a Pollster," *Washington Post*, October 16, 1988, p. C1; and Michael R. Kagay, "In Judging Polls What Counts Is When and How Who Is Asked What," *New York Times*, September 12, 1988, p. A16.

42. Irving Crespi, "The Case of Presidential Popularity," in A. Cantril, ed., *Polling on the Issues* (Cabin John, Md.: Seven Locks Press, 1980), p. 470.

43. E. J. Dionne, Jr., *New York Times*, January 27, 1987, p. A1.

44. Ibid.

45. David S. Broder, Haynes Johnson, and Paul Taylor, *Washington Post*, April 22, 1987.

46. *New York Times*, July 4, 1986.

47. *New York Times*, January 19, 1988.

48. Harris Poll news release, November 10, 1988.

49. Gallup Poll news release, November 6, 1988.

50. *Washington Post*, November 9, 1988, p. 1.

51. *New York Times*, November 9, 1988, p. A25.

52. Ibid., p. A1.

53. "Polls Show No Clear Consensus Among Voters About Direction New President Should Take," *Wall Street Journal*, November 9, 1988, p. A24.

54. Ibid.

55. Ibid.

56. Roshco, *Newsmaking*, pp. 34–35.

57. Ibid., p. 125.

58. Bogart, *Silent Politics*, p. 60.

59. Ibid., p. 61.

60. Philip Meyer, *Precision Journalism: A Reporter's Introduction to Social Science Methods* (Bloomington: Indiana University Press, 1973).

61. *New York Times*, January 19, 1988, and June 28, 1988.

62. Michael Oreskes and Robin Toner, *New York Times*, January 29, 1989, p. E5.

63. Michael Kagay, talk given at the American Association for Public Opinion Research Conference, St. Petersburg, Florida, May 20, 1989.

64. Irwin A. Lewis, talk given at the American Association for Public Opinion Research Conference, St. Petersburg, Florida, May 20, 1989.

CHAPTER 5: POLLS IN THE SERVICE OF DEMOCRACY

1. Benjamin Ginsberg, *The Captive Public: How Mass Opinion Promotes State Power* (New York: Basic Books, 1986), pp. 73–75.

INDEX